easy baby knits

easy baby knits

clothes & accessories
for 0–3 year-olds

claire montgomerie
photography by **claire richardson**

RYLAND
PETERS
& SMALL
LONDON NEW YORK

designer Pamela Daniels
editors Rachel Lawrence
  and Kate Haxell
location research Jess Walton
production Gordana Simakovic
art director Anne-Marie Bulat
publishing director Alison Starling

First published in the USA in 2007
by Ryland Peters & Small, Inc.
519 Broadway, 5th Floor
New York, NY 10012
www.rylandpeters.com

Text, design, and photographs
© Ryland Peters & Small 2007

10 9 8 7

ISBN-13: 978-1-84597-355-1
ISBN-10: 1-84597-355-0

Printed in China

Library of Congress Cataloging-in-Publication Data

Montgomerie, Claire.
  Easy baby knits : clothes & accessories for 0-3
year-olds / Claire
Montgomerie ; photography by Claire
Richardson.
     p. cm.
  Includes index.
  ISBN 978-1-84597-355-1
  1. Knitting--Patterns. 2. Infants' clothing. 3.
Children's clothing. I.
Title.
  TT825.M662 2007
  746.43'2041--dc22

                                    2006037463

contents

introduction

Babies' garments are the perfect starting point for anybody who is learning to knit. Aside from the obvious delight in seeing the miniature finished article on a tiny, precious baby, projects for little ones are much smaller than almost anything that would be knitted for adults and so you are far less likely to feel overwhelmed by the amount of work involved. The cute and simple patterns in this book are designed to be fun to knit and the projects gradually introduce new techniques, so you can progressively boost your knowledge and confidence in your ability. The patterns are supported by clear step-by-step technique instructions at the front of the book, making this a handy manual to which a novice knitter can refer.

As a textiles designer, conscious of the long history of knitting, I love vintage knits and have taken some inspiration from more traditional children's clothes from the last century to compile a group of patterns with a charm that is timeless and yet altogether modern. This book demonstrates the reason why hand-knitted items used to be a favorite gift for newborn babies and will inspire the beginner to experience the pleasure of giving a present made with their own hands. The patterns are comfortable and easy to wear, bearing in mind the wriggling restlessness of adventurous youngsters. The projects are original, fun, and in some cases, frivolous, with toys, accessories, and beautiful clothes all demonstrating that hand knitting does not have to produce lumpy, itchy sweaters with different-length sleeves! The yarns suggested are not scratchy wools or uncomfortable synthetics, but luxurious blends that are a pleasure to work with and great next to baby's soft skin. They are also, importantly, machine-washable—ideal for new parents with little time for hand washing.

Easy Baby Knits aims to banish the assumption that knitting is a hobby for a generation gone by, and to demonstrate that simple patterns need not be boring or plain to look at. As a knitting teacher I have seen how beginners assume some techniques to be much harder than they really are. Give these patterns a go and you may be pleasantly surprised by what you can accomplish. Once you have made one piece, mastering a new technique, you will be itching to progress onto the next project.

CLAIRE MONTGOMERIE

getting started

marker pins

buttons

row counter

essential equipment

The most important tools of the trade for knitters are obviously knitting needles and yarn, but there is a wide range of non-essential equipment that can help you enormously depending on the pattern you are attempting. However, we will begin with the fundamentals.

KNITTING NEEDLES

Needles come in many materials, such as bamboo, metal, plastic, casein, and different types of wood. I recommend bamboo needles for beginners as they are more pliable than needles made from other materials and so are kinder on your hands. Also, their texture causes the stitches to cling to them more than with other needles, so there is less chance of accidents, such as dropped stitches. Bamboo needles, rather than smooth metal or plastic, are also very often easier for the clammy hands of a novice knitter to grip! The choice of needles is ultimately down to personal preference, as the material does not affect the appearance of the stitches. However, it can affect your gauge, so don't change to a different type of needle halfway through a project. Some knitters like to use smooth metal needles with wool yarns and bamboo needles with silky, cotton yarns.

Knitting needles also come in different lengths, in order to accommodate different numbers of stitches. Some knitters prefer to use long needles almost exclusively, to tuck under their arm as they knit, or to prop them against their hip. Again, this is a personal preference and your style will emerge as you develop your technique. The size of needle you choose is determined by the weight (or thickness) of the yarn you are using. The needle size refers to the diameter of the needle; generally, thicker yarns need bigger needles. A recommended needle size will usually be shown on the ball band of your chosen yarn.

| stopper | stitch holder | stitch marker |

OTHER EQUIPMENT

Other essential items are a pair of sharp embroidery scissors, a tape measure, and a darning needle with a blunt tip for sewing up seams and weaving in ends of yarn. Stitch holders are very handy for keeping un-worked stitches safe until they are needed. The best kind are double-ended, so that you can knit the stitches straight off the holder instead of placing them back on the needle, but you can even use safety pins to hold small amounts of stitches safely.

A row counter is a non-essential, but is handy if you find counting rows confusing. Stoppers are another dispensable item, but they are great for stopping the stitches falling off the needle in your bag or workbox if you are in the middle of a project. Stitch markers are helpful for marking a position in your work that you will have to refer back to, such as where you have to begin to sew in a sleeve. Marker pins are useful for holding seams together and blocking and usually have larger heads than regular pins so that they don't get lost or pass through the stitches. Some knitted pieces need buttons and it is worth spending time choosing ones that work well on the garment you have put time and effort into making. Finally, a crochet hook is a great tool in dropped-stitch emergencies!

YARNS

There is currently a great array of wonderful yarns available, both natural and man-made. Natural yarns, made from animal and plant fibers are, as a rule, more pleasant to wear and easier to knit with, whereas man-made yarns are often cheaper, more durable, and easier to care for. As this is a book for babies, the yarns have been chosen carefully with them in mind. All the yarns used are machine-washable and many have a mixture of natural and man-made fibers in order to utilize the best qualities of both: the softness, warmth, and breathability of the natural fibers with the durability and easy care of the man-made.

Yarns come in varying weights and textures. The most common weights are lace, fingering, sport, DK/light worsted, worsted/Aran, chunky, and bulky. The thickness of a yarn is defined by the number of strands (or plies) spun together to make it, but as the thickness of the plies can vary, two yarns of the same weight, but of different brands, may not be exactly the same thickness.

The plies can be spun tightly or loosely to create different qualities, such as softness from a loose twist or strength from a tight twist. If you are a beginner, be careful with loose twists as the points of the needles can sometimes go through the yarn instead of through the stitch. The spinning process can also create textured yarns such as slub, gimp, bouclé, and other fancy types, which can create wonderful textures when knitted but can also be far more difficult for a novice to work with, so again be careful with these. Novelty yarns, such as ribbon, eyelash, furry, and metallic yarns, should also be treated with caution at first, as the stitches can be hard to define and so it is easier to make a mistake.

pulling yarn from the inside

PULLING YARN FROM THE INSIDE

When beginning a project, it is advisable that the working end of the yarn is taken from the inside of the ball, as shown in the picture, right. This stabilizes the ball of yarn. If the outside end is used, it can result in the ball rolling around too much and eventually knotting. It can be fussy digging out the inside end, but it is worth finding and using it, although if your efforts fail, the outside end will do the same job.

COUNTING ROWS

It is easy to lose track of which row you are on while knitting, but it is just as easy to count the rows already worked. In stockinette stitch each "V" shape is one stitch. Therefore, if you count up a vertical row of these, the number of "V"s is the number of rows. In garter stitch each ridge is two rows, so count each of these ridges and multiply by two to reach the number of rows.

holding
the needles
and yarn

There are no hard-and-fast rules to finding a comfortable way of knitting, but if you follow my suggestions on these pages, you will find that you can keep a steady pace and even gauge when knitting.

Here, I have shown two of the most common ways of holding the needles: like a pen (Method 1), or like a knife (Method 2). You may find that both hands want to hold the needles in the same way, or you might find that your right hand wants to hold the needle like a pen and the left hand like a knife, or vice versa, which is fine, too. Shown below right is a way of holding the yarn that will help you achieve an even gauge when knitting. It involves wrapping the yarn in a certain way around your right hand; it may be fiddly to master at first but it is important and will make things easier in the long run. However, bear in mind that there are different ways to hold the needles and yarn, and as long as you find a way that works for you, it will be the right way.

Remember that even if you are left-handed you can knit in this way, as both the left and right hands are involved fully in knitting.

Method 1 Holding the needle like a pen.

Method 2 Holding the needle like a knife.

Holding yarn The ball end of the yarn is wrapped around the little finger to control the speed of the yarn feeding through to the needle and so ultimately the gauge of the knitting. The yarn then passes under the two middle fingers and over the forefinger.

making a slip knot

Now that you are holding the needles and yarn comfortably, you are ready to begin knitting. The first thing to learn is how to make a proper slip knot.

When you are casting on the first row of stitches, you need to begin by making a slip knot, which will also be your first stitch. A slip knot is basically what it sounds like—a neat knot that can slip to the correct size to fit around any needle. When making this knot you will need to leave a tail of yarn from the loose end of the ball, a tail that will vary in length depending on the type of cast on you use (see pages 16–19).

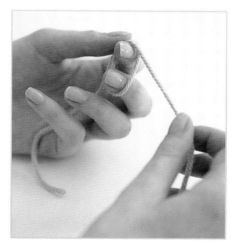

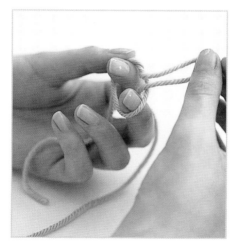

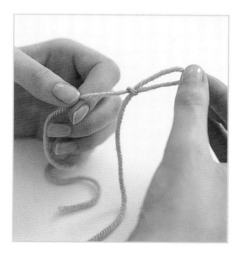

1 Wrap the ball end of the yarn around your first two fingers to create a ring and hold it in place with your thumb.

2 From the ball end of the yarn, pull a loop through the ring.

3 Holding the loop and loose end of yarn tightly, pull firmly to tighten the slip knot. You can now put a needle through this loop and pull one end of the yarn to tighten the loop to fit the diameter of the needle.

casting on: thumb method

There are many different ways of casting on, but here I am going to show you two of the neatest and most useful techniques, which are all you need to know to knit any of the projects in this book.

As you develop as a knitter, you can search out other techniques, especially if a complicated pattern requests a specific cast on method. Before casting on for your first project, spend some time practicing by casting on as many stitches as you can and then pulling them off and starting again until you feel that you have cracked the technique. It is often easy to forget how to do it, as you only cast on once right at the beginning of a piece, and it may be some time before you need to cast on again for another project.

This first technique is my preferred cast on method. It only uses one needle, effectively utilizing the thumb of your left hand as the other needle, and is especially neat and elastic. I recommend that you use this method for the initial cast on for all the projects in this book.

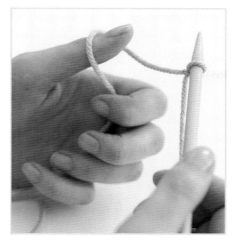

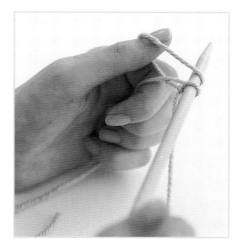

1 Make a slip knot, leaving a tail of yarn before it about three times the width of the cast on edge. This is something you will get better at judging with practice. Slip the knot onto a needle in your right hand and tighten it to the right size.

2 Grab the loose end of the yarn in your left hand and make a loop around your left thumb, as shown, still holding on tight to the loose end.

3 With your left thumb upright, pass the needle under the loop, from bottom to top.

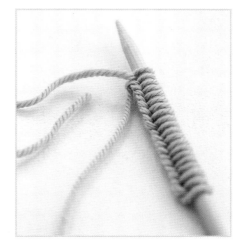

4 With your right hand, wrap the ball end of the yarn around the needle, passing the yarn underneath and then over the point. Hook the loop on your thumb over the point of the needle, as shown here.

5 Pull gently on the loose end of the yarn to draw the loop closely around the needle. Your first cast on stitch is complete and, together with the slip knot, you now have two stitches on the needle.

6 Repeat from Step 2, winding the yarn around your thumb to make the next stitch, and continue in this way until you have the correct number of stitches on the needle. When you begin to knit the first row, remember to use the ball end of the yarn to knit with, not the loose end.

casting on **17**

casting on: two-needle method

The two-needle method, or cable method as it is also known, of casting on is used in this book when you have to increase by many stitches at the end of a row or over a buttonhole.

If you find that you prefer the look or process of casting on using this method, you may, of course, use this technique to cast on any of the edges in this book. When a pattern does not specify how you must cast on, you can use your favorite method. For this cast on you will be holding one needle in each hand and the tail of yarn left before the slip knot only needs to be long enough to weave it in at the end—about 6–8in. long.

1 Make a slip knot, ensuring that you leave a tail long enough to weave in. Slip the knot onto the needle in your left hand and pull to tighten it.

2 Holding the ball end of the yarn in your right hand, insert the right-hand needle from front to back into the loop.

3 With your right hand, wrap the ball end of the yarn around the needle, passing the yarn underneath and then over the point.

4 Using the tip of the right-hand needle, draw the yarn looped over the needle through the original slip knot. You should now have a loop on each needle.

5 Place the new loop on the right-hand needle onto the left-hand needle to create a second stitch. Pull gently on the ball end of the yarn to tighten and neaten the stitch.

6 Your first cast on stitch is complete and, together with the slip knot, you now have two stitches on the needle.

7 For the next and every other stitch, place the needle from front to back between the two previous stitches. Repeat from Step 3, wrapping the yarn around the needle, but drawing the loop through between the two stitches before placing it onto the left-hand needle.

8 Repeat the process until you have the correct number of cast on stitches on the left-hand needle.

garter stitch

knit stitch

The knit stitch is the simplest of all stitches. To practice obtaining the perfect gauge and the actions used in knitting, cast on some stitches and knit every row until you feel you have learned the basic technique. Knitting every row forms the ridged fabric called garter stitch (see picture, above). This is the simplest fabric to work up and is the same on both sides, so it makes for a great scarf, which is why the Baby Scarf on page 42 is an excellent first project to try. In knitting you hold the needle with the stitches on in your left hand and transfer them all to the right-hand needle by knitting a row. It will all become clear with the basic knit stitch.

1 Hold the needle with the stitches on in your left hand. Insert the right-hand needle into the first stitch on the left-hand needle from left to right and front to back.

2 Holding the yarn at the back of the work, with your right hand wrap the ball end of the yarn around the right-hand needle, passing the yarn underneath and then over the point.

3 Using the tip of the right-hand needle, draw the yarn looped over the needle through the stitch on the left-hand needle.

4 Keeping the new loop on the right-hand needle, slip the first stitch off the left-hand needle. Repeat these steps until all the stitches are transferred onto the right-hand needle. This completes a knit row. Swap the needles in your hands and start the next row.

stockinette stitch

purl stitch

Once you have learned to purl you know all the stitches you need to knit anything. Every other technique is a combination or slight variation on knit and purl stitches. Working alternate rows of knit and purl stitches forms stockinette stitch, the most recognized knitted fabric (see picture, above). The side of the fabric showing is called the right side and is smooth, formed of stitches that look like a "V." To help you keep track of whether you are on a knit or purl row while knitting stockinette stitch, remember that whenever this (right) side is facing you on the left-hand needle, you must knit the next row.

The other side of the fabric is called reverse stockinette stitch and resembles garter stitch, but without the ridges: you can see this reverse side in the step pictures on the right. When this side is facing you on the left-hand needle, you must purl the next row, as shown in the steps.

1 Hold the needle with the stitches on in your left hand. Insert the right-hand needle through the front of the first stitch on the left-hand needle from right to left.

2 Holding the yarn at the back of the work, with your right hand wrap the ball end of the yarn around the right-hand needle, passing the yarn over and around the point.

3 Using the tip of the right-hand needle, draw the yarn looped over the needle back through the stitch on the left-hand needle.

4 Keeping the loop on the right-hand needle, slip the first stitch off the left-hand needle. Repeat until all the stitches are on the right-hand needle. This completes a purl row. Swap the needles in your hands and start a knit row to work stockinette stitch.

sizing

Throughout this book the sizing for a project is given at the top of the pattern. With no standard sizes for babies, and a huge variation in newborn baby weights and growth in young children, we have used an average size for each age and given the actual measurements of the finished garment underneath. This allows you to choose the size of the garment you want to make by comparing its finished size with the size of the child it is for. In this way, even if you have a taller, lighter, or smaller than average child, you can make a garment that will fit them— or that they can grow in to! (I'm sure you don't want to spend days making something that will only fit for a week.)

Even if you want to make the garment for the child to wear now, remember to allow some room for movement: don't knit the chest size that is exactly the child's measurement and take time getting your gauge right (see opposite), to ensure that your garment will be as close as possible to the size you chose.

gauge

A gauge swatch is used to ensure that you are knitting to the gauge called for in the pattern. This is essential in order to achieve the right size garment, so please do take the time to knit a swatch or you may be disappointed with your finished project. To work a gauge swatch, knit a square about 5 x 5in. using the needles, yarn, and pattern stated in the gauge instructions. Lay the swatch flat and, keeping away from the edges, measure and mark out 4in. (10cm) with marker pins. Count the number of stitches between the pins. Then repeat the process in the other direction to count the number of rows.

If you find you have more stitches than required, then your gauge is too tight. Don't try to knit more loosely as everyone has a natural gauge and you won't be able to keep your stitches consistent. Instead, try again with bigger needles. If there are fewer stitches than required, then your gauge is too loose and you need to decrease the size of the needles.

Don't worry if your gauge is not correct first time, knitting is not a precise art and everybody tends to knit to a different gauge. For projects where a good fit is not required, such as some accessories and toys, you need not complete a swatch unless you want to ensure the size.

rib stitch

Rib is used in a knitted garment in areas that need to be more elastic, such as cuffs. Rib retains its structure after stretching, meaning that the cuff will open up to let a hand through but will then spring back to its narrower dimension.

Rib is made up of a combination of knit and purl stitches next to each other. When working rib you are using knit and purl stitches in the same row, so you will be using the working end of yarn at both the back and front of the work. This means transferring the working yarn from back to front, or front to back, between stitches. These steps demonstrate this on 1x1 rib stitch, which is knit 1, purl 1—abbreviated as "k1, p1"—across the row.

1x1 rib stitch

1 Here a knit stitch has just been worked, meaning that the yarn is being held at the back of the knitting.

WORKING RIB STITCH

Moving the yarn back and forth in this way may sound tricky, but once you start you will very quickly pick up the rhythm. In the pictures below the points of the needles have been separated so you can see clearly what is happening. However, once you get used to the stitch pattern you will find that you hardly have to open the needles at all to move the yarn.

The difficulty most people have in learning rib is keeping track of which stitch you need to work next. If you look closely at Step 2, below left, you will see that the next stitch to be worked on the left-hand needle has a little bar of yarn across it at the base. This indicates that on the previous row it was knitted, so on this row you have to purl it. In Step 4, below right, you can see that the next stitch to be worked does not have the bar of yarn, so you must knit it. After a few rows the columns of knit and purl stitches will be obvious, making it easier to see which stitch is needed next.

2 To work the next stitch, a purl stitch, the yarn must be at the front of the work. To move it to the right position, just bring it forward between the needles.

3 Now work a purl stitch in the usual way, holding the yarn at the front.

4 Before working the next stitch, a knit stitch, return the yarn between the needles to the back. In the next row, all the stitches that were knitted must be purled and vice versa. So if you end a row with a purl stitch, you must begin the next row with a knit stitch.

variations of rib technique

Once you have mastered the technique of passing the yarn between the needles to the other side of the work, you can work any combination of knit and purl stitches across a row to create other stitch patterns.

2x2 rib stitch

Rib can appear in many different forms, of which the 1x1 rib you have learned is the simplest. A common and attractive version is 2x2 rib, shown right, above. This pattern is formed by knitting two stitches, then purling the following two and repeating this across the row. It is abbreviated as "k2, p2." This version is popular in garments as the rib can be more easily seen: 1x1 rib, when not at full stretch, can often look like stockinette stitch. Once you know how to do 2x2 rib, you can experiment with different multiples of knit and purl, such as 3x3 or 6x6.

Another variation of rib technique is seed stitch. This is a very pretty stitch that is sometimes called moss stitch. It looks more complicated than it is, which is great for a beginner and is why it is used often in this book. If you can rib, you can seed. A seed stitch usually uses an odd number of stitches and starts with a 1x1 rib row (k1, p1) across the row, with the last stitch being knitted. However, on the next row, all the stitches that were knitted must be knitted and those that were purled, purled. This is why an odd number of stitches is helpful, as you know that you will always start and end a row with a knit stitch. Each row will be exactly the same and is written as, "k1 *p1, k1; rep from * to end." If you decide that you have to use an even number of stitches, just remember to keep to the rule of knitting the knits and purling the purls. If you lose track of which stitch to work next, you should also be able to see what to do from the pattern that is emerging; all the purl stitches appear as protruding "seeds," which will help you to see what the next stitch should be.

seed stitch

increasing

Knitted garments are usually made of shaped pieces, because if you had to cut shapes and sew them together the edges would be untidy and would unravel. Therefore, shaping must be incorporated as you work. Again, as with casting on, there are several different ways of increasing, but the main differences are purely cosmetic, and so to begin with I am showing you just one increase technique, which is written as "inc into next st." This can be used anywhere within a row to obtain different shaping. However, this process can only increase a few stitches at a time, the most common amount being just one at a time. If you need to increase more stitches at the end of a row you will have to cast them on using the two-needle method, which is shown on page 18.

1   Insert the right-hand needle into the stitch, wrap the yarn around and draw it through as normal, but do not drop the original stitch off the left-hand needle. Pull the needles apart to make more room in the loop on the left-hand needle.

2   Insert the right-hand needle into the back of the loop on the left-hand needle, from front to back. Wrap the yarn around it with your right hand as if you were knitting normally and draw a second loop through onto the right-hand needle.

3   Now drop the original stitch off the left-hand needle to complete the increase. Two stitches have been made from the one original stitch, so one stitch has been increased.

Increasing by casting on This method can only be used at the end of a row. For example, you will use it to increase for arms when knitting a sweater in one piece.

decreasing

As with increasing, there are different decrease techniques, but here I have shown two of the most common. The difference between the two lies in the direction in which they slant. Knit two together, "k2tog," slants to the right on a knit row, while slip one, knit one, pass slipped stitch over, "sl 1, k1, psso," slants to the left. You can use them at opposite ends of the same row to create a decorative edge. Both these techniques can only decrease a few stitches at a time. If you need to decrease more stitches at the start or end of a row you will have to cast them off using the basic bind off shown on page 30.

K2tog: 1 Knit to the position of the decrease; here it is being worked at the start of a row. Insert the right-hand needle through the front loops of the next two stitches from front to back.

2 Wrap the yarn around the right-hand needle as normal and then just knit the two stitches as if they were one. One stitch has been decreased.

Sl1, k1, psso: 1 Knit to the position of the decrease; here it is being worked at the start of a row. Slip one stitch by inserting the right-hand needle into the stitch purlwise (from right to left), and then slipping it from the left-hand needle onto the right-hand needle, without knitting it.

2 Knit the next stitch as normal.

3 Using the tip of the left-hand needle, lift the first (slipped) stitch on the right-hand needle over the second (knitted) stitch and then drop it right off the right-hand needle, leaving only one stitch on the right-hand needle. One stitch has been decreased.

binding off

Binding off uses both needles and it is very easy when you are learning to knit to get the gauge wrong. It is common for beginners to bind off too tightly, drawing in the top of the fabric. If you find this happens, it is essential that you correct it by practicing knitting more loosely on the bind off, or even by using a larger set of needles just for the bind off.

1   On the bind off row, knit the first two stitches as normal.

2   Insert the tip of the left-hand needle into the first stitch on the right-hand needle.

3   Pull the first stitch up and lift it over the second stitch.

4 Drop the first stitch off the right-hand needle so that only one stitch remains on this needle. To progress along the row, knit the next stitch from the left-hand needle, so that once again you have two stitches on the right-hand needle. Repeat from Step 2, lifting the first stitch over the second one. Repeat until there is just one stitch on the right-hand needle.

5 Gently pull on the right-hand needle to increase the size of the last stitch to a large loop. Remove the needle and cut the yarn, leaving a 6–8in. tail.

6 Slip the cut end of the yarn through the loop. Pull on the end of the yarn to tighten the loop into a knot and secure the bound off edge.

useful techniques

JOINING IN BALLS/STRIPES

When you have run out of yarn you must join in a new ball: the method used is the same for joining in a new color if you are striping. In both cases you should join in the new yarn at the beginning of a row.

Insert the right-hand needle into the next stitch as normal. Leaving a 6–8in. tail, loop the end of the new yarn over the tip of the right-hand needle, draw it through, and drop the original stitch. You have made one stitch with the new yarn. Knit the next few stitches as normal, then go back and gently pull the first stitch taut and tie the two ends of yarn in a loose knot to secure them.

If you are joining in a different color at the beginning of a row to work stripes, you need not cut off the yarn and tie in a new color every time you begin a new stripe. Carry the color not in use loosely up the edge of the work, twisting it with the other color at the end of the row until you need to use it again.

However, if you are making wide stripes this twisting technique can begin to look untidy. If the edge will not be hidden in a seam, if you are knitting a scarf perhaps, it may be better to join in new yarn each time you begin a new stripe and then weave in the loose ends neatly when you have finished all the knitting.

PICK UP AND KNIT

Sometimes you have to pick up some stitches from the edge of a completed piece of knitted fabric in order to knit another part of the project. This is simple to do and the pattern will tell you where on the knitted fabric you need to pick up from.

With the right side of the fabric facing you, put the tip of a needle through the middle of the first stitch to be picked up from. At the back, loop the end of a ball of yarn (leaving a 6–8in. tail), over the tip of the needle, then draw this loop through the knitted fabric. Repeat in the next stitch along, or as instructed in the pattern, until you have picked up the required number of stitches. Then you just knit the stitches following the pattern instructions. Weave in the loose end of yarn neatly when the knitting is complete.

BUTTONHOLES

Buttonholes can be worked quite easily within knitting by binding off a certain number of stitches on one row, then casting them on again in the next.

1 On a knit row, knit to the position of the buttonhole. Bind off the number of stitches stated in the pattern, or enough to accommodate the button you want to use. Continue knitting to the end of the row.

2 Purl to the buttonhole. Turn the work around and cast on the same number of stitches as were bound off in the previous row. Turn the work back and purl on the other side of the buttonhole to the end of the row. Buttonhole complete.

EYELET/LACE HOLES

The eyelet hole is easy to create and is commonly used to make small buttonholes in baby clothes.

If you work eyelets throughout a piece of knitting a lace effect is achieved. The lace squares in the Naming Day Blanket on page 104 look pretty and complicated, but are actually composed of a relatively simple repetition of eyelet holes.

1 Knit to the position of the eyelet. Bring the yarn between the needles to the front (yo), then knit the next two stitches together (k2tog). This decrease cancels out the increase made by bringing the yarn over. On the next row knit the yarn over loop as if it were a normal stitch.

2 To make lace patterns, continue to work eyelet holes as in Step 1 (yo, k2tog), at even intervals across the row. Here you can see how the gaps made are evident even as you are knitting the row. Knit or purl the next row in the normal way before working more eyelets.

finishing

The finishing of a garment is often something knitters dread as good finishing is not noticed but bad finishing is glaringly obvious. However, if you learn to do it correctly, finishing is very satisfying.

WEAVING IN ENDS

Never ever cut the loose ends of yarn left at the edges of your knitting to less than 6–8in. long or they may slip through the stitches and unravel. Untie knots holding two ends of yarn together before weaving the ends in. Thread a large-eyed darning needle or a knitter's sewing needle with the tail of yarn and follow either of the two methods shown (right, above), to weave the tail into the back of the knitted fabric. The needle needs to be blunt in order to make sure that the point does not pass through the strands of yarn, which can become messy.

REINFORCING FOR SNAPS

With a child's garment it is essential that you sew on any buttons or snaps tightly so that they do not come loose and become a choking hazard. Due to the stretchy nature of knitted fabric, any area to which snaps are to be attached should be reinforced so that the action of fastening the garment does not pull it out of shape or rip the yarn. You can do this by sewing the snaps to a length of petersham ribbon or bias tape and then sewing this to the garment, ensuring that it is concealed.

Method 1 Thread the needle and yarn through the loops along the edge of the work for about 2–3in., then sew back through a few of the last loops to secure the yarn.

Method 2 Thread the needle and yarn through stitches, inserting the needle through the top of the loop on the first stitch then through the bottom on the next for about 2–3in. along. Sew back through a few of the last loops to secure.

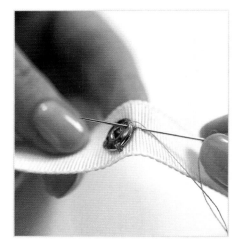

Reinforcing for snaps Sew the snaps to a piece of ribbon or bias tape using a sewing needle and thread. Using the same needle and thread and neat oversewing stitches, sew the tape to the back of the garment where the fastening needs to be.

Blocking Before you sew up a garment it is worth blocking the pieces to get the best possible finish. Lay the piece on a padded surface (an ironing board is ideal), and carefully pin it flat, easing it into the right shape. Press it following the instructions on the yarn ball band.

SEWING SEAMS

Bad finishing is very noticeable on seams, so mattress stitch, sewn using a blunt needle, is the best way to join them. In a stockinette stitch or ribbed fabric this is invisible if worked correctly, as you can see at the bottom of the seam being sewn in the picture, right. Always use the same color yarn as in the main body of work (here a contrast color has been used to help you clearly see what is happening), so that as the seams are pulled and moved when the garment is worn, the joining yarn cannot be seen. Some yarns may be too weak to sew up a seam, so double these up, add a stronger yarn to the original one, or use a different yarn altogether, but ensure it is a similar color.

Mattress stitch With the right sides of both pieces of knitting to be joined facing you, secure the yarn at the bottom of one piece with small stitches on the back. Bring the needle through to the front at the bottom, between the edge stitch and the next stitch in. Take the needle across to the other piece and pick up two loops between the edge stitch and the next stitch:

you can see the loops on the needle in the picture above. Pull the yarn through and pull it taut. Take the needle back to the first piece, insert it where it exited and pick up two loops. Continue in this way, going from one side to the other, as if lacing up a corset, until you reach the last stitch. Secure the yarn on the back with a few small stitches.

fixing mistakes

There are many mistakes to be made in knitting and it is odd how beginners frequently make the same ones.

When knitting straight, beginners often end up with slanting edges caused by either gaining or losing stitches. While you may think it is more common to lose stitches, it is actually more common to gain them. To avoid this, try to count your stitches at the start of every row as you work to see if you can spot where the mistake has been made. Be careful not to pass the yarn from front to back when it is not called for, do not wrap the yarn twice around the needle when knitting, and always remember to drop the final loop at the end of a stitch. The best thing to do when learning is to take it very slowly and try not to get distracted—watching television while working is for experienced knitters! By counting the stitches at the beginning of a row you will hopefully avoid the common beginner's mistake of counting the first stitch as two: as the edge stitches can be quite loose when you are inexperienced, they can often be twisted and look like two separate stitches.

It is inevitable as a beginner that you will drop stitches—even experts cannot completely avoid this mistake. However, dropped stitches are nearly as easy to fix as they are to make. The steps opposite show you how to pick up a dropped stitch with your knitting needles. Once you have mastered the principle, try doing this with a small crochet hook as it is quicker and easier when you know how.

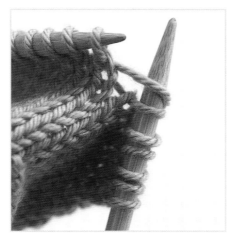

1 This picture shows what a dropped stitch looks like. If left, it will drop further down the rows to form a ladder. If this occurs you must pick up each strand of the ladder, from lowest first, to account for each row.

2 Firstly, slip the dropped stitch loop onto the right-hand needle. With the tip of the same needle, pick up the lowest strand of yarn in the ladder, taking the needle under the strand from front to back.

3 Slip the stitch loop over the strand and off the end of the right-hand needle. The strand has become the new stitch loop. Continue in this way until all the strands in the ladder have been picked up. Slip the final stitch loop onto the left-hand needle, ready to knit.

reading patterns

At first glance, patterns can seem like they are written in a foreign language. However, on closer inspection, you will see that they are mainly composed of abbreviations and if you know what each one is short for, you can read the pattern as you would an ordinary piece of writing. It may be helpful to go through a new pattern first, just to ensure that all the abbreviations and techniques used are familiar to you and to save you having to look anything up during the making.

As you read through a pattern, don't be put off if it seems very complicated. When you are actually knitting it, the pattern language should become much clearer and just by working through the instructions manually you will be able to understand what they mean more fully. A list of the abbreviations used in this book is given opposite.

The most important abbreviations are "k" for knit and "p" for purl. These abbreviations will generally be next to a number to indicate how many stitches need to be knitted or purled. For example, "k2" means "knit two stitches." The other important symbols to look out for in a pattern are commas, asterisks, and brackets.

Commas separate single instructions; for example, "k1, p2" means "knit one stitch, purl the next two stitches." Asterisks are placed to indicate a section in a pattern that is repeated more than once; the number of repetitions will be specified further along in the row. For example, "k1, *p1, k1; rep from * to end" means "knit the first stitch, and then purl then knit alternate stitches until you reach the end of the row."

Square brackets are used to enclose instructions that need to be worked a number of times, with the number of times needed written immediately after the closing bracket. For example, "[k1, p2] 8 times" is telling you, "knit one stitch, then purl two stitches and repeat this sequence eight times in total." Round brackets are used in listing the instructions for different sizes in a pattern; the smallest size is listed before the opening bracket, then all the other sizes are inside the brackets, with the largest size last. Where there are many different sizes you may find it helpful to circle with a pencil all the instructions for your particular size before you start knitting. Numbers in italics at the end of a row are the stitch count—the number of stitches you should have on the needle after finishing the row. Again, numbers in brackets are for larger sizes.

abbreviations

alt	alternate
beg	beginning
cont	continue
dec	decrease
foll	following
inc	increase
k	knit
p	purl
patt	pattern
PM	place marker
psso	pass slipped stitch over
rem	remaining
rep	repeat
RS	right side
sl	slip
st(s)	stitch(es)
st-st	stockinette stitch
tbl	through the back loops (of the stitch)
tog	together
WS	wrong side
yo	yarn over

baby clothes

baby scarf

The easiest pattern for a beginner is a scarf: you cast on some stitches and then just knit until it is the required length, so it is a great opportunity to practice your technique. This scarf is knitted in garter stitch (every row knit)—the simplest fabric to make.

If you want to make it even simpler, knit it in one color.

The great thing about this pattern is that it is adaptable. You can knit different-width stripes, make the scarf longer or shorter, cast on different numbers of stitches, or use thicker yarn. The beauty is that whatever size the finished scarf is, it will fit!

This basic pattern can also be used to make scarves for adults. Just cast on more stitches and knit more rows. You can also use a bulkier or more textured yarn, but remember to change needle size if you do so.

gauge

25 sts and 42 rows to 4in. measured over garter stitch using Rowan Cashsoft DK on size 6 needles, or the size required to give the correct gauge.

Always check gauge carefully and adjust needle size if necessary (see page 23).

measurements

LENGTH   33in.

WIDTH   5in.

Each stripe measures 3in.

scarf

Using size 6 needles and yarn A, cast on 30 sts.

Knit 30 rows.

Fasten off yarn A.

Join in yarn B.

Knit 30 rows.

Fasten off yarn B.

Cont in this way, knitting 30 rows of each color alternately until 11 stripes in all have been made, ending with a stripe of yarn A.

Bind off.

to finish

Weave in all ends.

materials

1 1¾oz (50g) ball of Rowan Cashsoft DK
   in shade 503 (yarn A)
1 1¾oz (50g) ball of Rowan Cashsoft Baby
   DK in shade 809 (yarn B)
Pair of size 6 knitting needles
Darning needle

abbreviations

See page 39

baby papoose

This papoose has been designed as an extremely

easy-to-make, simple-to-use blanket to keep baby warm.

Creating a hood makes the papoose easier to wrap baby

in after a bath or before a trip outdoors. The incredibly soft,

warm yarn will keep baby cosy from head to toe.

materials

2 1¾oz (50g) balls of Debbie Bliss
    Cashmerino Aran in shade 104 (yarn A)
6 1¾oz (50g) balls of Debbie Bliss
    Cashmerino Aran in shade 002 (yarn B)
Pair of size 8 knitting needles, 14in. long,
    or work back and forth on a size 8
    circular needle
Darning needle

abbreviations

See page 39

The papoose is knitted with the cast on edge along one side rather than at the bottom, which means that you may need longer needles than usual to fit on the 160 stitches. We used 14-in. long needles for this project.

gauge

20 sts and 38 rows to 4in. measured over garter stitch using Cashmerino Aran on size 8 needles, or the size required to give the correct gauge.

Always check gauge carefully and adjust needle size if necessary (see page 23).

measurements

LENGTH 32in.
WIDTH 24in.

papoose

Using size 8 needles and yarn A, cast on 160 sts.

Work 1¹⁄₂in. in garter stitch (every row knit), ending with a WS row.

Fasten off yarn A.

Join in yarn B.

Work in garter st until work measures 22in. from cast on edge, ending with a WS row.

Fasten off yarn B.

Rejoin yarn A.

Work in garter st until work measures 24in. from cast on edge, ending with a WS row.

Bind off.

to finish

Press lightly and weave in all ends.

Fold top two corners to center (see diagram, right) and sew seam neatly, matching edge stripe on either side, to make hood.

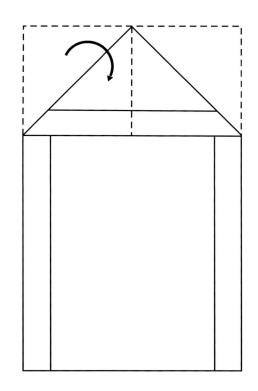

Fold in the top corners of the knitted rectangle so that they meet. Sew up the short seam to create the pointed hood.

simple sweater

Sweaters are generally regarded as difficult to make, but this

one is a very basic shape and has simple instructions. While I don't

recommend that a beginner choose this as their first ever project—a

simple blanket or scarf is much better for practicing technique and

gauge—this is a good pattern for a first attempt at a sweater.

The sweater is knitted entirely in garter stitch, from the bottom

upward, with the sleeves and body worked together. This also makes

the sweater appear to knit up quickly as there are only two pieces—

a front and a back—to be made!

materials

3 1¾oz (50g) balls of GGH Merino Soft
   in shade 79 (yarn A)
1 1¾oz (50g) ball of GGH Merino Soft
   in shade 78 (yarn B)
Pair of size 5 knitting needles
Stitch holder
Darning needle
3 small buttons

abbreviations

See page 39

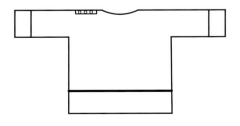

gauge

27 sts and 36 rows to 4in. measured over garter stitch on size 5 needles, or the size required to give the correct gauge.

Always check gauge carefully and adjust needle size if necessary (see page 23).

measurements

TO FIT	0–3	3–6	6–9	9–12	12–18 months
CHEST	20	21	23	24	25½in.
LENGTH	9½	10¼	11	12	12¾in.
SLEEVE	6	6¾	8	9	10in. (before turn back)

back

**Using size 5 needles and yarn B, cast on 68(73:78:83:88) sts.

Work 2(2½:3:3:3)in. in garter st (every row knit), ending with a WS row.

Fasten off yarn B.

Join in yarn A.

Cont in garter st for a further 4(4:4:4½:4¾)in., ending with a WS row, then cast on 40(46:52:58:64) sts at the end of this last row for the right sleeve. *108(119:130:141:152) sts.*

Next row (RS): Knit across cast on sts and 68(73:78:83:88) sts of body, then cast on 40(46:52:58:64) sts at end of row for the left sleeve. *148(165:182:199:216) sts.*

Next row (WS): Knit across all 148(165:182:199:216) sts.**

Work on these sts for a further 3½(4:4½:4¾:5)in., ending with a WS row.

SHAPE NECK AND SHOULDERS

With RS facing, k57(65:73:81:89) sts and leave these stitches on a holder for right sleeve, then bind off next 34(35:36:37:38) sts for back neck, knit to end. *57(65:73:81:89) sts on needle for left sleeve.*

Knit 2 rows on these 57(65:73:81:89) sts.

Bind off.

With WS facing, rejoin yarn A to inner (neck) edge of right sleeve stitches on holder and knit all 57(65:73:81:89) sts from holder.

Next row (outer edge of sleeve): Bind off 40(46:54:62:68) sts, knit to end. *17(19:19:19:21) sts on needle.*

Knit 3 rows on these 17(19:19:19:21) sts.

Bind off.

front

Work as given for Back from ** to **.

Work on these 148(165:182:199:216) sts for a further 3(3¾:4:4½:4¾)in., ending with a WS row.

SHAPE NECK AND SHOULDERS

With RS facing, k61(69:77:85:93) sts and leave these sts on a holder for left sleeve, then bind off 26(27:28:29:30) sts for front neck, knit to end. *61(69:77:85:93) sts on needle.*

Work on these 61(69:77:85:93) sts for front right neck and right sleeve.

SHAPE RIGHT SIDE OF NECK

1st row (WS): Knit to last 3sts, k2tog, k1. *60(68:76:84:92) sts.*

2nd row: K1, k2tog, knit to end. *59(67:75:83:91) sts.*

3rd row: Knit to last 3sts, k2tog, k1. *58(66:74:82:90) sts.*

4th row: K1, k2tog, knit to end. *57(65:73:81:89) sts.*

5th row: Bind off 40(46:54:62:68) sts for right sleeve, knit to end. *17(19:19:19:21) sts.*

6th row: Knit.

7th row (buttonhole row): K2(3:3:3:4), yo, k2tog, k4, yo, k2tog, k4, yo, k2tog, k1(2:2:2:3). (3 buttonholes made.)

8th row: Knit.

Bind off.

SHAPE LEFT SIDE OF NECK

With WS facing, rejoin yarn A to right neck stitches left on the holder and starting at neck edge, knit all stitches from holder as follows:

1st row: K1, k2tog, knit to end. *60(68:76:84:92) sts.*

2nd row: Knit to last 3 sts, k2tog, k1. *59(67:75:83:91) sts.*

3rd row: K1, k2tog, knit to end. *58(66:74:82:90) sts.*

4th row: Knit to last 3 sts, k2tog, k1. *57(65:73:81:89) sts.*

Bind off.

to finish

Sew seams at top of sleeves, leaving the button and buttonhole bands on right shoulder unsewn.

Sew side and under-sleeve seams, ensuring that the color change is straight all around body and reversing the seam for the turnback at the cuff.

Weave in all ends.

Sew three buttons to button band corresponding with buttonholes.

cotton and wool hats

A simple and easy hat pattern is a fantastic way to practice shaping

and to produce a practical and adorable final product fairly quickly.

These hats also demonstrate how you can adapt a pattern by

working stripes, adding accessories such as a pompom, or by

changing the stitches around the edge: here the cotton hat

has a garter stitch edge and the wool hat has a ribbed edge.

Changing the type of yarn illustrates how you can make a hat

suitable for cold (wool) or warmer (cotton) weather.

The pattern for the cotton hat is given on these pages, the wool hat is on pages 58–59. When knitting these patterns, feel free to mix and match, by making the wool hat stripy or adding a pompom to the cotton one. Alternatively, as you become more experienced, you can use this very basic pattern and add your own flourishes.

gauge

20 sts and 28 rows to 4in. measured over stockinette stitch using Debbie Bliss Cotton DK on size 6 needles, or the size required to give the correct gauge.

Always check gauge carefully and adjust needle size if necessary (see page 23).

measurements

TO FIT   0–3   3–6   6–12   12–18   18–24   24–36 months

cotton hat

Using size 6 needles and yarn A, cast on 66(74:82:90:98:106) sts.

Work 6 rows garter st (every row knit).

Drop yarn A.

Join in yarn B.

Starting with a purl (WS) row, work 2 rows st-st.

Drop yarn B.

Pick up yarn A.

Starting with a purl (WS) row, work 2 rows st-st.

Cont in st-st, working in stripes of 2 rows in yarn B and two rows in yarn A throughout until 3$\frac{1}{2}$(4:4$\frac{1}{2}$:5:5$\frac{1}{2}$:6)in. st-st have been worked in all, ending with a purl row.

SHAPE TOP

Maintain stripe pattern throughout.

1st row (RS): [K6(7:8:9:10:11), k2tog] 8 times, k2. *58(66:74:82:90:98) sts.*

2nd row: Purl.

3rd row: [K5(6:7:8:9:10), k2tog] 8 times, k2. *50(58:66:74:82:90) sts.*

4th row: Purl.

5th row: [K4(5:6:7:8:9), k2tog] 8 times, k2. *42(50:58:66:74:82) sts.*

6th row: Purl.

Cont in this way, working one stitch less between decreases and purling every other row until

materials

1 1$\frac{3}{4}$oz (50g) ball of Debbie Bliss Cotton
   DK in shade 19 (yarn A)
1 1$\frac{3}{4}$oz (50g) ball of Debbie Bliss Cotton
   DK in shade 09 (yarn B)
Pair of size 6 knitting needles
Darning needle

abbreviations

See page 39

18 sts remain, ending with the purl row.

Next row: [K2tog] 9 times. *9 sts.*

Break off yarn, leaving approx 20in. for sewing up. Thread yarn through rem 9 sts and pull tight to make a ring.

to finish

Sew seam using mattress stitch, being careful to match stripes. Fasten off yarn.

Weave in all ends.

Press lightly to shape.

materials

1 (1, 1, 1, 2, 2) 1¾oz (50g) balls of Rowan
Cashsoft DK in shade 501 (yarn A)
1 1¾oz (50g) ball of Rowan Cashsoft DK
in shade 502 (yarn B)
Pair of size 6 knitting needles
Darning needle

abbreviations

See page 39

gauge

25 sts and 30 rows to 4in. measured over stockinette stitch using Rowan Cashsoft DK on size 6 needles, or the size required to give the correct gauge.

Always check gauge carefully and adjust needle size if necessary (see page 23).

measurements

TO FIT   0–3   3–6   6–12   12–18   18–24   24–36 months

wool hat

Using size 6 needles and yarn B, cast on 76(86:96:106:116:126) sts.

1st row: *K1, p1; rep from * to end.

Repeating 1st row forms 1x1 rib.

Work 5 more rows in 1x1 rib.

Fasten off yarn B.

Join in yarn A.

Starting with a purl (WS) row, cont in st-st for 3(3½:4:4½:4¾:5)in., ending with a purl row.

SHAPE TOP

1st row (RS): [K5(6:7:8:9:10), k2tog] 10 times, k6. *66(76:86:96:106:116) sts.*

2nd row: Purl.

3rd row: [K4(5:6:7:8:9), k2tog] 10 times, k6. *56(66:76:86:96:106) sts.*

4th row: Purl.

5th row: [K3(4:5:6:7:8), k2tog] 10 times, k6. *46(56:66:76:86:96) sts.*

6th row: Purl.

Cont in this way, working one stitch less between decreases and purling every other row until 26 sts remain, ending with the purl row.

Next row: [K2tog] 13 times. *13 sts.*

Break off yarn, leaving approx 20in. for sewing up. Thread yarn through rem 13 sts and pull tight to make ring.

to finish

Sew seam using mattress stitch, being careful to match ribbed stripe. Fasten off yarn.

Weave in all ends.

Press lightly to shape.

Using yarn B, make a small pompom and attach it to the top of the hat.

simple bootees and scratch mitts

These bootees and scratch mitts are designed for newborn

babies. The bootees are sock style—easy to pull on, but hard for

baby to pull off! The mitts are great for preventing newborn

babies scratching themselves, but can also be knitted in

a larger size to use as regular mittens for slightly older babies.

materials

1 1¾oz (50g) ball of Debbie Bliss Baby
    Cashmerino in shade 001
Oddments of white yarn for pompoms:
    we used Baby Cashmerino in shade 101
Pair each of size 2 and size 3 knitting
    needles
Darning needle
1yd of ¼-in. wide ribbon

abbreviations

See page 39

To knit a pair of mitts and matching bootees should take only one ball of
Debbie Bliss Baby Cashmerino.

gauge

28 sts and 34 rows to 4in. measured over stockinette stitch using Debbie Bliss Baby
Cashmerino on size 3 needles, or the size required to give the correct gauge.
Always check gauge carefully and adjust needle size if necessary (see page 23).

measurements

TO FIT   newborn   3–6 months

bootees

Start at the sole.
Using size 3 needles, cast on 36(52) sts.
1st row (WS): Knit.
2nd row: Inc in first st, k13(21), [inc in next st, k1] 4 times, knit to last 2 sts, inc in next st, k1.
42(58) sts.
3rd row: Knit.
4th row: Inc in first st, k16(24), [inc in next st, k1] 4 times, knit to last 2 sts, inc in next st, k1.
48(64) sts.
5th row: Knit.
6th row: Inc in first st, k19(27), [inc in next st, k1] 4 times, knit to last 2 sts, inc in next st, k1.
54(70) sts.
Work 7(13) rows in garter stitch without shaping.

DIVIDE FOR INSTEP
1st row (RS): K24(32), sl 1, k1, psso, k2, k2tog, k4, k2tog, turn. Leave rem unworked sts on
the needle.
2nd row: Sl 1, k12, k2tog, turn. Leave rem unworked sts on the needle.
3rd row: Sl 1, k3, sl 1, k1, psso, k2, k2tog, k4, k2tog, turn.
Rep 2nd and 3rd rows 3(5) times.
Next row: As 2nd row.
Next row: Knit to end across worked and unworked sts.
Next row (WS): Knit to end across all sts. *34(42) sts.*
Change to size 2 needles and work the ribbed top.
1st row (RS): K2, *p2, k2; rep from * to end.
2nd row: P2, *k2, p2; rep from * to end.
1st and 2nd rows form 2x2 rib.

Rep 1st and 2nd rows until rib measures 3(3¼)in.

Bind off.

to finish

Press lightly on WS.

Sew seam, reversing seam 1¼(1½)in. from top of ribbed section to allow for turnover. Turn top edge back to RS.

Make two small pompoms and attach one to each instep.

scratch mitts

Using size 2 needles, cast on 30(34) sts.

1st row (RS): K2, *p2, k2; rep from * to end.

2nd row: P2, *k2, p2; rep from * to end.

1st and 2nd rows form 2x2 rib.

Rep 1st and 2nd rows until rib measures 1(1¼)in., ending with a 2nd row.

Change to size 3 needles.

Next row (RS): Knit.

Next row (eyelet row): K2(1), *yo, k2tog, k3(2); rep from * 4(7) times, k3(1).

Work in garter stitch for a further 1½(2)in., ending with a WS row.

SHAPE TOP

1st row (RS): [K1, k2tog tbl, k9(11), k2tog, k1] twice. *26(30) sts.*

2nd and every alternate row: Knit.

3rd row: [K1, k2tog tbl, k7(9), k2tog, k1] twice. *22(26) sts.*

5th row: [K1, k2tog tbl, k5(7), k2tog, k1] twice. *18(22) sts.*

7th row: [K1, k2tog tbl, k3(5), k2tog, k1] twice. *14(18) sts.*

8th row: Knit.

Bind off.

to finish

Press lightly on WS.

Sew seams.

Weave in all ends.

Thread ribbon through eyelet holes. Tie bow and secure with a holding stitch if you don't wish it to untie.

cotton bootees

There are two versions of these cute bootees, to suit either

boys or girls. The knitting pattern is slightly more complicated

than previous patterns in this book, but it should be

manageable for a beginner. The bootees are very quick to

make and each pair needs only one ball of yarn.

materials

1 1¾oz (50g) ball of Debbie Bliss Cotton
   DK in shade 16 or shade 19

Pair of size 5 knitting needles

Stitch holders

Darning needle

2 buttons

abbreviations

See page 39

Knit the first part of the pattern—the basic shoe shape—for both the t-bar and side-strap versions of the bootees, then choose the second part of the pattern according to the version you prefer.

gauge

20 sts and 38 rows to 4in. measured over garter stitch using Debbie Bliss Cotton DK on size 5 needles, or the size required to give the correct gauge.

Always check gauge carefully and adjust needle size if necessary (see page 23).

measurements

TO FIT   0–6   6–12 months

bootees

Using size 5 needles, cast on 32(38) sts.

1st row: Knit.

DIVIDE FOR INSTEP

1st row: K21(25), turn, leaving last 11(13) sts on a stitch holder.

Work 12(16) rows on next 10(12) sts in basket weave pattern as follows:

1st row: K3, p2, k2, p2, k1(3), turn. Leave the rem 11(13) sts on a second stitch holder.

2nd row: P1(3), k2, p2, k2, p3, turn.

3rd row: K1(3), p2, k2, p2, k3, turn.

4th row: P3, k2, p2, k2, p1(3), turn.

Repeat last four rows 2(3) times more, but do not turn on last row.

Next row: Keeping the bootee and the knitting needles in the same position as they were at the end of the last row worked, pick up and knit 7(9) sts along side of basket weave panel just worked, then knit the 11(13) sts from the first stitch holder, turn. *28(34) sts.*

SHAPE FOOT

1st row: Knit the 28(34) sts just worked, then pick up and knit 7(9) sts along other side of basket weave panel and then knit the 11(13) remaining stitches from the second stitch holder. *46(56) sts.*

2nd to 8th (10th) rows: Knit.

Next row: Bind off 2(4) sts knit to end. *44(52) sts.*

Next row: Bind off 2(4) sts, k2, k2tog, k14(17), k2tog, k2, k2tog, k14(17), k2tog, k2. *38(44) sts.*

Next row: Knit.

Next row: K2, k2tog, k12(15), k2tog, k2, k2tog, k12(15), k2tog, k2. *34(40) sts.*

Next row: Knit.

Next row: K2, k2tog, k10(13), k2tog, k2, k2tog, k10(13), k2tog, k2. *30(36) sts.*

Bind off.

to finish

Press lightly on WS.

Sew seams.

Weave in all ends.

side strap bootees

Using size 5 needles, with RS of bootee facing, pick up and knit 8(10) sts evenly across top of back of the shoe, 4(5) sts either side of seam.

Turn and work 5(7) rows garter stitch on these 8(10) sts.

Next row: Cast on 4(5) sts for the right bootee or 20(22) sts for the left bootee, knit to end.

Next row: Cast on 20(22) sts for the right bootee or 4(5) sts for the left bootee, knit to end. *32(37) sts.*

Next row (buttonhole row):

For right bootee; knit to last three sts, yo, k2tog, k1.

For left bootee; k2, yo, k2tog, knit to end.

Next row: Knit.

Bind off.

Attach button to each short side of strap to fasten bootees.

t-bar bootees

Using size 5 needles, with front of bootee facing pick up and knit 3 sts at center top of front basket weave instep panel.

Work 5(7) rows garter stitch on these 3 sts. Do not bind off but leave these 3 sts on a stitch holder.

Using size 5 needles, with RS of bootee facing, pick up and knit 8(10) sts evenly across top of back of the shoe, 4(5) sts either side of seam.

Turn and work 5(7) rows garter stitch on these 8 sts.

Next row: Cast on 4(5) sts for the right bootee or cast on 9(10) sts, then knit 3 sts from holder, then cast on 9(10) sts for the left bootee, knit to end.

Next row: Cast on 9(10) sts then knit 3 sts from holder then cast on 9(10) sts for the right bootee or cast on 4(5) sts for the left bootee, knit to end. *33(38) sts.*

Next row (buttonhole row):

For right bootee; knit to last three sts, yo, k2tog, k1.

For left bootee; k2, yo, k2tog, knit to end.

Next row: Knit.

Bind off.

Attach button to each short side of strap to fasten bootee.

wrap top

An uncomplicated yet pretty pattern, this top is knitted entirely

in one piece, which helps the beginner with finishing as there is

little to do! There are fewer pieces to get confused about and

fewer seams to sew. When you split for the neck at the back,

instead of binding off, one side is continued until it is complete,

while the remaining side is placed on a holder and then worked

afterward. This may sound hard to accomplish, but it is, in fact,

an incredibly neat way to work. The tie waist detail is practical,

as well as being incredibly sweet, because there are no buttons to

do up while the little lady wriggles when being dressed.

gauge

23 sts and 33 rows to 4in. measured over stockinette stitch using Rowan Cashsoft DK on size 6 needles, or the size required to give the correct gauge.

Always check gauge carefully and adjust needle size if necessary (see page 23).

measurements

TO FIT	0–6	6–12	12–18	18–24	24–36 months
CHEST	20	22½	24	26	27½in.
LENGTH	9	9½	10¼	11	12in.

wrap top

Start at the bottom of the back. Using size 6 needles, cast on 58(66:72:76:80) sts.

Work 5 rows in garter st.

6th row (WS): Purl.

Work 5½(5½:6¼:6¾:7)in. in st-st, starting with a knit row and ending with a purl row.

Cont in st-st, inc one st at each end of the next row and every foll alt row to 66(74:80:84:88) sts, ending with a knit row.

SHAPE SLEEVES

1st row (WS): Cast on 16(16:16:18:18) sts, purl to end. *82(90:96:102:106) sts.*

2nd row: Cast on 16(16:16:18:18) sts, knit to end. *98(106:112:120:124) sts.*

3rd row: K3, purl to last 3 sts, k3.

4th row: Knit.

Rep 3rd and 4th rows until sleeve section measures 2½(2¾:2¾:3:3½)in., ending with a 4th row.

Next row (WS): K3, p32(35:38:41:42), k28(30:30:32:34), p32(35:38:41:42), k3.

Next row: Knit.

Rep the last two rows once more.

DIVIDE FOR FRONTS

Next row (WS): K3, p32(35:38:41:42), k3 and leave these 38(41:44:47:48) sts on a holder for left front, bind off 22(24:24:26:28) sts, k2, p32(35:38:41:42), k3. *38(41:44:47:48) sts on needle.*

right front

Continue working on the 38(41:44:47:48) sts on right-hand needle.

Next row (RS): Knit.

Next row: K3, p32(35:38:41:42), k3.

Rep last two rows once more.

Maintaining k3 border at sleeve edge and k3 border at neck edge on every row, cont in st-st inc 1 st at neck edge on every row inside the k3 border to 58(65:68:73:78) sts, ending with a WS row.

materials

2(2:3:3:4) 1¾oz (50g) balls of Rowan
   Cashsoft Baby DK in shade 807

Pair of size 6 needles

Stitch holder

Stitch markers

Darning needle

1yd of ½-in. wide ribbon

abbreviations

See page 39

SHAPE SLEEVE

Next row (RS): Bind off 16(16:16:18:18) sts, knit to last 4 sts, inc 1 st as before, k3. *43(50:53:56:61) sts.*

Maintaining the k3 border at neck edge, cont in st-st inc 1 st at neck edge as before on every row while at the same time dec 1 st at armhole on next RS row and every foll RS row until 4 decs in all have been worked. *46(53:56:59:64) sts.*

Maintaining the k3 border at neck edge, cont in st-st without further armhole shaping but continuing to inc at neck as before to 49(57:63:65:67) sts. Place marker at side edge on last row.

Maintaining the k3 border at neck (front) edge, continue in st-st without shaping until right front measures the same as the back to the garter stitch rows, ending with a RS row. Work 4 rows in garter st.
Bind off.

left front

Rejoin yarn to 38(41:44:47:48) sts on holder and work exactly the same as for right front, reversing all shapings and omitting marker.

to finish

Place a second marker on the right front ¾in. below the first marker.
Sew side seams with mattress stitch, leaving the right side seam open between the markers to thread ribbon through.
Remove markers.
Sew sleeve seams. Weave in all ends.
Attach two lengths of ribbon, one to each front, where shaping stops under neck.

baby bonnet

An adorable version of a traditional bonnet, this hat is perfect

all year round, prettily protecting baby from the sun in the

summer and keeping him cozy in the winter. Although it

may seem a more feminine item, bonnets have traditionally been

worn by baby boys and girls and this one is simple enough to

suit both, particularly for a special occasion like a naming

ceremony or spring wedding. The ties under the chin will stop

baby from tugging the bonnet off.

gauge

28 sts and 34 rows to 4in. measured over stockinette stitch using Debbie Bliss Baby Cashmerino on size 3 needles, or the size required to give the correct gauge.

Always check gauge carefully and adjust needle size if necessary (see page 23).

measurements

TO FIT   0–3   3–6   6–12 months

bonnet

Start at front edge.

Using size 3 needles, cast on 225 sts.

1st row: K1, *p1, k1; rep from * to end.

Repeating 1st row forms seed stitch.

Work 3 more rows in seed st.

Next row: Bind off 73(70:67) sts in seed st, k79(85:91) sts, bind off rem 73(70:67) sts in seed st.

Rejoin yarn to main body of hat.

Work 2¾(3:3½)in. in st-st, beg with a knit row and ending with a purl row.

SHAPE BACK

1st row (RS): *K11(12:13), k2tog; rep from * to last st, k1. *73(79:85) sts.*

Work 3 rows st-st.

5th row: *K10(11:12), k2tog; rep from * to last st, k1. *67(73:79) sts.*

6th row: Purl.

Cont in this way, working one stitch less between decreases and purling every other row until 13 sts remain, ending with the dec row.

Next row: Purl.

Next row: [K2tog] 6 times, k1. *7 sts.*

Break off yarn, leaving approx 20in. for sewing up. Thread yarn through rem 7 sts and pull tight to make ring.

materials

1 1¾oz (50g) ball of of Debbie Bliss Baby
    Cashmerino in shade 101

Pair of size 3 knitting needles, 14in. long

Darning needle

abbreviations

See page 39

to finish

Sew 1½in. of seam using mattress stitch.

Fasten off yarn.

Weave in all ends.

Press lightly to shape.

neckband

With RS facing, join yarn to edge of st-st next to seed st tie and pick up and knit 50(56:62) sts around bottom edge of bonnet.

1st row (WS): *K1, p1; rep from * to end.

1st row repeated forms 1x1 rib.

Work 3 more rows in 1x1 rib.

Bind off in rib.

cardigan

This basic pattern for a versatile cardigan is an essential garment

for a young baby. It can be worn at any time of the year,

particularly if you knit a version in summer-weight cotton.

The pretty seed stitch edging in a contrast color is an easy way

of making a simple pattern look more complicated and

interesting. Of course, if you wish you can knit the whole thing

in one color and omit the ribbon to create a very unfussy, classic

look, especially appropriate if you are knitting for a boy.

materials

2(3:3:4:5) 1¾oz (50g) balls of Rowan
 Cashsoft Baby DK in shade 502 (yarn A)

1 1¾oz (50g) ball of Rowan Cashsoft Baby
 DK in shade 504 (yarn B)

Pair of size 6 knitting needles

Stitch holder

Darning needle

1¾yd of ¾-in. wide petersham ribbon
 or bias tape

4 medium snaps

Approx 12in. of ¾-in. wide ribbon

abbreviations

See page 39

gauge

23 sts and 33 rows to 4in. measured over stockinette stitch using Rowan Cashsoft Baby DK
on size 6 needles, or the size required to give the correct gauge.

Always check gauge carefully and adjust needle size if necessary (see page 23).

measurements

TO FIT	3–6	6–12	12–18	18–24	24–36 months
CHEST	20	22½	25	27	28½in.
LENGTH	9½	10¼	11	12	12¾in.
SLEEVE SEAM	6	6¾	7¼	8½	9in.

back

Using size 6 needles and yarn B, cast on 57(65:73:77:81) sts.

1st row: K1, *p1, k1; rep from * to end.

Repeating 1st row forms seed st.

Work 3 more rows in seed st.

Fasten off yarn B.

Join in yarn A.

Work 6(6¼:6¾:7:8)in. in st-st, beg with a knit row and ending with a purl row.

SHAPE ARMHOLES

Bind off 3(4:4:5:5) sts at beginning of next 2 rows. *51(57:65:67:71) sts.*

Dec one st at each end of the next row and foll 0(1:2:2:3) alt rows. *49(53:59:61:63) sts.*

Cont in st-st without shaping until back measures 9(10:10¾:11½:12¼)in., ending with a purl row.

SHAPE NECK AND SHOULDER HOLES

1st row (RS): K10(12:14:14:15), k1, *p1, k1; rep from * over next 26(26:28:30:30) sts,
k10(12:14:14:15).

2nd row: P10(12:14:14:15), k1, *p1, k1; rep from * over next 26(26:28:30:30) sts,
p10(12:14:14:15).

Rep 1st and 2nd rows once more.

5th row: K10(12:14:14:15), seed st 4 and leave these 14(16:18:18:19) sts on a holder for right
back neck, bind off 21(21:23:25:25) sts, seed st 3, k10(12:14:14:15). *14(16:18:18:19) sts on
right-hand needle.*

6th row: P10(12:14:14:15), seed st 4.

7th row: Seed st 4, knit to end.

Bind off in patt.

Rejoin yarn to rem sts and work one row to match other shoulder.

Bind off.

left front

Using size 6 needles and yarn B, cast on 31(35:39:43:45) sts.

1st row (RS): K1, *p1, k1; rep from * to end.

Repeating 1st row forms seed st.

Work 3 more rows in seed st.

Fasten off yarn B.

Join in yarn A.

Next row: Knit to last 4 sts, p1, k1, p1, k1.

Next row: Seed st 4 sts, purl to end.

Rep the last 2 rows for 6(6¼:6¾:7:8)in.
in all, ending with a WS row.

SHAPE ARMHOLE

Maintain the 4 sts seed st border at front edge.

1st row (RS): Bind off 3(4:4:5:5) sts, knit to last 4 sts, seed st 4. 28(31:35:38:40) sts.

2nd row: Seed st 4, purl to end.

Dec one st at armhole edge end on the next row and on foll 0(1:2:2:3) alt rows. *27(29:32:35:36) sts.*

Cont in st-st with 4 sts seed st front border without shaping until left front measures 8(8¾:9½:10¼:11)in., ending with a RS row.

SHAPE NECK

1st row (WS): Seed st 17(17:18:21:21) sts, purl to end.

2nd row: Knit to last 17(17:18:21:21) sts, seed st to end.

Rep 1st and 2nd rows once more.

5th row: Bind off 13(13:14:17:17) sts in seed st, seed st 4, purl to end. *14(16:18:18:19) sts.*

6th row: K10(12:14:14:15) sts, seed st 4.

7th row: Seed st 4, purl to end.

Rep 6th and 7th rows until left front measures 9½(10¼:11:12:12¾)in. from cast on edge.
Bind off.

right front

Using Size 6 needles and yarn B, cast on 31(35:39:43:45) sts.

1st row: K1, *p1, k1; rep from * to end.

Repeating 1st row forms seed st.

Work 3 more rows in seed st.

Fasten off yarn B.

Join in yarn A.

Next row (RS): K1, p1, k1, p1, knit to end.

Next row: Purl to last 4 sts, seed st 4.

Rep the last 2 rows for 6(6¼:6¾:7:8)in.
in all, ending with a RS row.

SHAPE ARMHOLE

Maintain the 4 sts seed st border at front edge.

1st row (WS): Bind off 3(4:4:5:5) sts, purl to last 4 sts, seed st 4. *28(31:35:38:40) sts.*

2nd row: Seed st 4, knit to end, dec 1 st at armhole edge. *27(30:34:37:39) sts.*

Dec one st at armhole edge on the foll 0(1:2:2:3) alt rows. *27(29:32:35:36) sts.*

Cont in st-st with 4 sts seed st front border without shaping until right front measures 8(8¾:9½:10¼:11)in., ending with a WS row.

SHAPE NECK

1st row (RS): Seed st 17(17:18:21:21) sts, knit to end.

2nd row: Purl to last 17(17:18:21:21) sts, seed st to end.

Rep 1st and 2nd rows once more.

5th row: Bind off 13(13:14:17:17) sts in seed st, seed st 4, knit to end. *14(16:18:18:19) sts.*

6th row: P10(12:14:14:15) sts, seed st 4.

7th row: Seed st 4, knit to end.

Rep 6th and 7th rows until right front measures 9½(10¼:11:12:3¾)in. from cast on edge.
Bind off.

sleeves (both alike)

Using size 6 needles and yarn B, cast on 29(31:33:35:37) sts.

1st row: K1, *p1, k1; rep from * to end.

Repeating 1st row forms seed st.

Work 3 more rows in seed st.

Fasten off yarn B.

Join in yarn A.

Beg with a knit row, work 4 rows in st-st.

Inc 1 st at either end of row and every foll 8th(6th:5th:5th:5th) row until 39(47:53:59:61) sts.

Cont in st-st without shaping until sleeve measures 6(6¾:7½:8¼:9)in. from cast on edge.

SHAPE TOP

Bind off 3(4:4:5:5) sts at beg of next two rows, then dec 1 st at each end on next row and on foll 0(1:2:2:3) alt rows. *31(35:39:43:43) sts.*

Purl 1 row.

Bind off.

to finish

Press all pieces lightly.

Sew shoulder seams with mattress st.

Fold sleeves in half lengthwise. Matching center top of sleeve to shoulder seam, sew sleeves into armholes.

Join side and sleeve seams with mattress stitch.

Weave in all ends.

With WS of the cardigan facing, stitch strips of petersham ribbon or bias tape along the length of both front edgings—this will help reinforce the edgings.

Attach snaps to the reinforced edging, at evenly spaced intervals.

Attach ribbon to outside front edge, if needed.

knitted dress

A very simple-to-make and easy-to-wear dress, this pattern is

timeless in its shape and style. The dress is pretty enough to

please the girliest of girls, and yet so unfussy and comfortable

that a tomboy will love to play in it. The dress is also easily

adaptable for girls of varying heights. If your child is unusually tall

or short for her age, you can adjust the length by knitting more

or fewer rows after the decreasing in the skirt, without having to

change the body measurements.

materials

2(3:3:3) 1¾oz (50g) balls of Debbie Bliss
    Cashmerino Aran in shade 603 (yarn A)

1(2:2:2) 1¾oz (50g) balls of Debbie Bliss
    Cashmerino Aran in shade 617 (yarn B)

Pair of size 8 knitting needles

Stitch holder

Darning needle

2 buttons

1yd length of ¾-in. wide ribbon if desired

abbreviations

See page 39

gauge

21 sts and 27 rows to 4in. measured over stockinette stitch using Debbie Bliss Cashmerino Aran on size 8 needles, or the size required to give the correct gauge.

Always check gauge carefully and adjust needle size if necessary (see page 23).

measurements

TO FIT	6–12	12–18	18–24	24–36 months
CHEST	20½	22	24	25¼in.
LENGTH	15¾	17½	18	19in.

front

**Using size 8 needles and yarn B, cast on 65(69:73:77) sts.

1st row: K1, *p1, k1; rep from * to end.

Repeating 1st row forms seed st.

Work 3 more rows in seed st.

Fasten off yarn B.

Join in yarn A.

5th row (RS): Knit.

6th row: Purl.

Repeating 5th and 6th rows forms st-st.

Work 8(10:12:12) more rows in st-st, beg with a knit row and ending with a purl row.

Next row (RS): Knit, dec 1 st at each end of the row. *63(67:71:75) sts.*

Cont in st-st, beg with a purl row, dec 1 st at each end of every following 12th(12th:14th:16th) row 4 times. *55(59:63:67) sts.*

Cont in st-st without shaping until front measures 11½(12¼:12¾:13)in. from cast on edge, ending with a knit row.

Fasten off yarn A.

Join in yarn B.

Next row (WS): Purl.

Next row (RS): K1, *p1, k1; rep from * to end.

Rep last row until seed st section measures 1½(1½:2:2)in., ending with a WS row.

SHAPE ARMHOLES

Maintain continuity of seed st throughout.

Bind off 3(4:4:5) sts at beg of next 2 rows. *49(51:55:57) sts.*

Dec 1 st at each end of next 4(3:3:2) rows. *41(45:49:53) sts.*

Cont in seed st without shaping until seed st measures 3(3½:4:4½)in., ending with WS row.**

SHAPE NECK

Maintain continuity of seed st throughout.

Next row (RS): Seed st 10(11:12:13) and leave these sts on a holder for left side of neck, bind off next 21(23:25:27) sts, seed st 9(10:11:12). *10(11:12:13) sts on right-hand needle.*

Work a further 1¼(1½:1½:1½)in. in seed st on these 10(11:12:13) sts, ending with a WS row.

Bind off.

LEFT SIDE OF NECK

Rejoin yarn B to 10(11:12:13) sts left on a holder and work to match right side of neck.

Bind off.

back

Work as front from ** to **.

SHAPE NECK

Maintain continuity of seed st throughout.

Next row (RS): Seed st 10(11:12:13) and leave these sts on a holder for right side of neck, bind off next 21(23:25:27) sts, seed st 9(10:11:12). *10(11:12:13) sts on right-hand needle.*

Work a further 1¼(1½:1½:1½)in. in seed st on these 10(11:12:13) sts, ending with a WS row.

Next row (first buttonhole row): Seed st 4(4:5:5), bind off next 2 sts, seed st to end.

Next row (second buttonhole row): Seed st 4(5:5:6), cast on 2 sts, seed st to end.

Buttonhole made.

Work 2 rows in seed st.

Bind off.

RIGHT SIDE OF NECK

Rejoin yarn B to 10(11:12:13) sts left on a holder and work a further 1¼(1½:1½:1½)in. in seed st on these 10(11:12:13) sts, ending with a WS row.

Next row (first buttonhole row): Seed st 4(6:5:6) bind off next 2 sts, seed st to end.

Next row (second buttonhole row): Seed st 4(4:5:5) cast on 2 sts, seed st to end.

Buttonhole made.

Work 2 rows in seed st.

Bind off.

to finish

Press lightly and weave in all ends.

Sew side seams with mattress stitch.

Weave in all ends.

Sew buttons onto front straps to correspond with buttonholes on back straps. The straps are meant to overlap completely, which will help you place the buttons, but you may adjust where to place them.

Attach a ribbon to the empire-line waist, where yarn A meets yarn B, if desired. It may help to just sew it at one side seam to secure it, and then you can tighten or loosen it when you tie it into a bow.

overalls

These nautical-style overalls are perfect for baby to play in.

The legs are long enough to cover the diaper and keep baby

warm, but short enough for some serious playtime without the

worry of flapping trouser legs. This makes the overalls

especially great for babies who are just learning to crawl.

The underleg section opens to allow for diaper changing and is

fitted with no-nonsense snaps. With the unavoidable wear this

part of the garment will receive, it is recommended that you

reinforce it with tape, such as bias tape, on either side of

the opening to ease the strain.

materials

3(3:4) 1¾oz (50g) balls of Debbie Bliss
    Cashmerino Aran in shade 202 (yarn A)

1(1:2) 1¾oz (50g) ball of Debbie Bliss
    Cashmerino Aran in shade 102 (yarn B)

1(1:2) 1¾oz (50g) ball of Debbie Bliss
    Cashmerino Aran in shade 207 (yarn C)

1(1:2) 1¾oz (50g) ball of Debbie Bliss
    Cashmerino Aran in shade 001 (yarn D)

Pair of size 8 knitting needles

Stitch holder

Darning needle

2 large buttons

5 snaps

½yd petersham ribbon or bias tape

abbreviations

See page 39

gauge

18 sts and 24 rows to 4in. measured over stockinette stitch using Debbie Bliss Cashmerino
Aran on size 8 needles, or the size required to give the correct gauge.

Always check gauge carefully and adjust needle size if necessary (see page 23).

measurements

TO FIT	3–6	6–9	9–12 months
CHEST	20	22½	24in.
LENGTH FROM SHOULDER TO TOP OF LEG	12	14	16½in.

front

**Using size 8 needles and yarn A, cast on 14(16:18) sts.

Work 5 rows st-st beg with a knit (RS) row.

Cont in st-st, casting on 5(6:6) sts at the end of the next row and foll 3 rows and then 6(6:6)
sts at the end of the foll 4 rows. *58(64:66) sts.*

Work 15 rows in st-st without shaping, beginning and ending with a purl row. PM at each end
of first row to mark the end of the leg shaping.

Cont in st-st, dec 1 st at each end of the next row and on every foll 4th(6th:8th) row to
46(52:54) sts.

Cont in st-st without shaping until front measures 6¾(8¼:10)in. from top of leg shaping,
ending with a purl row.

Fasten off yarn A.

CHANGE TO STRIPE PATTERN

Cont in st-st.

Join in yarn B.

Work one row.

Drop yarn B.

Join in yarn C.

Work one row.

Drop yarn C.

Join in yarn D.

Work one row.

Drop yarn D.

SHAPE ARMHOLES

Cont in st-st maintaining the continuity of the three-row stripe pattern.

The colors will not need to be fastened off but can be carried up the side of the work.

Dec 1 st at each end of the next row and every foll row to 36(42:44) sts.

Cont in st-st without shaping until the striped section measures 2¾(3½:4½)in., ending with a knit row.

Next row: P10(12:12), k16(18:20), p10(12:12).

Next row: Knit.

Next row: P10(12:12), k16(18:20), p10(12:12).**

DIVIDE FOR STRAPS

Next row: K10(12:12) sts and leave these sts on a holder for the second strap, bind off 16(18:20) sts, k9(11:11). *10(12:12) sts on right-hand needle.*

Next row (WS): K2, purl to last 2 sts, k2.

Next row: Knit.

Rep the last 2 rows until the strap measures 1½(2:2)in., ending with a WS row.

Bind off.

Rejoin yarn to stitches left on the holder for the second strap, and complete to match first strap.

back

Work as for front from ** to **.

DIVIDE FOR STRAPS

Next row: K10(12:12) sts and leave these sts on a holder for the second strap, bind off 16(18:20) sts, k9(11:11). *10(12:12) sts on right-hand needle.*

Next row (WS): K2, purl to last 2 sts, k2.

Next row: Knit.

Rep the last 2 rows for ¾in., ending with a WS row.

Next row (first buttonhole row): K4(5:5), bind off 2 sts, k3(4:4).

Next row (second buttonhole row): K2, p2(3:3), cast on 2 sts, p2(3:3), k2.

Cont in st-st in stripe patt until the strap measures 1½(2:2)in., ending with a WS row.

Bind off.

Rejoin yarn to stitches left on the holder for the second strap, and complete to match first strap.

Bind off.

leg bands (both alike)

Join side seams.

With RS facing, using size 8 needles and yarn A, pick up and knit 4 sts from side edge of underleg flap, 53(57:57) sts all round leg shaping and 4 sts along side edge of other underleg flap. *61(65:65) sts.*

1st row (WS): *P1, k1; rep from * to last st, p1.

2nd row: K1, *p1, k1; rep from * to end.

Repeating 1st and 2nd rows forms 1x1 rib.

Work 2 more rows in 1x1 rib.

Bind off in rib.

to finish

Weave in all ends.

Do not sew underleg seam. Sew petersham ribbon or bias tape along both facing flaps where they are to join, on the side which will not show.

Sew 4 or 5 snaps to the binding to fasten the overalls.

Sew buttons to straps corresponding with the buttonholes.

matinée jacket

A traditional gift for a new mother and baby has always been a

matinée jacket. Its simple beauty is still suitable for contemporary

bundles of joy. Use it as a cardigan, dress coat, or just a simple

dressing gown; it is versatile and lovely for any occasion.

This jacket looks extremely pretty, due to the textured seed

stitch, but is, in fact, very simple to make.

materials

3 (3:4) 1¾oz (50g) balls of Rowan Cashsoft Baby
   DK in shade 801

Pair of size 6 knitting needles

Darning needle

Stitch holder

3 buttons

abbreviations

See page 39

gauge

23 sts and 33 rows to 4in. measured over stockinette stitch using Rowan Cashsoft Baby DK
on size 6 needles, or the size required to give the correct gauge.

Always check gauge carefully and adjust needle size if necessary (see page 23).

measurements

TO FIT	0–3	3–6	6–12 months
CHEST	17½	21	24in.
LENGTH	9½	10¼	12¾in.
SLEEVE SEAM	4¾	6	7in.

back

Using size 6 needles, cast on 73(87:92) sts.

Work 5(7:7) rows in garter stitch.

Next row (WS): Purl.

Work in st-st until back measures 5½(6:8)in., ending with a RS row.

SHAPE YOKE

Next row (WS): *K2, k2tog; rep from * to last 1(3:0) sts, k1(3:0). *55(66:69) sts.*

FIRST TWO SIZES ONLY

Next row (RS): K2tog, k24(30), k3(2)tog, k24(30), k2tog. *51(63) sts.*

ALL SIZES

Work 4(4:5) rows in garter st without shaping.

CHANGE TO SEED STITCH PATTERN

1st row (WS): K1,*p1, k1; rep from * to end.

1st row repeated forms seed stitch.

Cont in seed st until back measures 9½(10¼:12¾)in., ending with a WS row.

SHAPE NECK

Next row: Patt 13(17:19) sts and leave these sts on a holder, bind off 25(29:31) sts, patt
12(16:18) sts. *13(17:19) sts on needle.*

Patt one row on these 13(17:19) sts.

Bind off in patt.

Rejoin yarn to 13(17:19) sts left on a holder.

Patt one row.

Bind off in patt.

left front

Using size 6 needles, cast on 42(48:54) sts.

Work 5(7:7) rows in garter st.

Next row (WS): K3, purl to end.

Next row: Knit.

Rep these two rows until left front measures 5½(6:8)in., ending with a RS row.

SHAPE YOKE

Next row (WS): *K1, k2tog; rep from * end. *28(32:36) sts.*

Work 5 rows in garter st without shaping.

CHANGE TO SEED STITCH PATTERN

1st row (WS): K3, p1, *k1, p1; rep from * to end.

Next row (RS): *P1, k1; rep from * to last 4 sts, p1, k3.

Rep the last two rows until left front measures 8½(9:11½)in., ending with RS row.

SHAPE NECK

Next row: Bind off 5(5:7) sts, patt to end. *23(27:29) sts.*

Maintaining continuity of pattern, decrease one st at neck edge on every row until 13(17:19) sts rem.

Work in patt on these 13(17:19) sts until left front measures 8(10¼:10¾)in., ending with a WS row.

Bind off in patt.

right front

Using size 6 needles, cast on 42(48:54) sts.

Work 5(7:7) rows in garter st.

Next row (WS): Purl to last 3 sts, k3.

Next row: Knit.

Rep these two rows until right front measures 5½(6:8)in., ending with a RS row.

SHAPE YOKE

Next row (WS): *K2 tog, k1; rep from * end. 28(32:36) sts.

Next row: Knit.

Next row (buttonhole row) (WS): Knit to last 3 sts, k1, yo, k2tog.

Work 3 rows in garter st.

CHANGE TO SEED STITCH PATTERN

1st row (WS): *P1, k1; rep from * to last 4 sts, p1, k3.

Next row (RS): K3, p1, *k1, p1; rep from * to end.

Rep the last two rows until right front measures 7(7½:9½)in., ending with a RS row.

Next row (buttonhole row) (WS): Patt to last 3 sts, k1, yo, k2tog.

Cont in patt as before until right front measures 8(8¾:11¼)in., ending with a RS row.

Next row (buttonhole row) (WS): Patt to last 3 sts, k1, yo, k2tog.

Cont in patt as before until right front measures 8¼(9:11½)in., ending with a WS row.

SHAPE NECK

Next row (RS): Bind off 5(5:7) sts, patt to end. *23(27:29) sts.*

Maintaining continuity of pattern, decrease one st at neck edge on every row until 13(17:19) sts rem.

Work in patt on these 13(17:19) sts until

right front measures 8(10½:12¾)in., ending with a RS row.

Bind off in patt.

sleeves (both alike)

Using size 6 needles, cast on 23(29:33) sts.

Work 4(6:6) rows in garter st.

1st row (WS): K1, *p1, k1; rep from * to end.

1st row repeated forms seed stitch.

Cont in seed st inc 1 st at each end of next row and every foll 4th row to 37(43:47) sts.

2ND AND 3RD SIZES ONLY

Cont in seed st inc 1 st at each end of every foll 6th row to (43:47) sts.

3RD SIZE ONLY

Cont in seed st inc 1 st at each end of every foll 8th row to (53) sts.

ALL SIZES

Cont in seed st without shaping until sleeve measures 4¾(6:7)in.

Bind off in patt.

to finish

Press all pieces lightly.

Using mattress st, sew shoulder seams.

Fold sleeves in half lengthwise. Matching center top of sleeve to shoulder seam, sew bound off edge of sleeve to seed st edge of main body.

Sew side and sleeve seams.

Weave in all ends.

Sew on three buttons to correspond with buttonholes.

double-breasted knit coat

Once you have mastered the basic stitches you can experiment

with them in different combinations to make new and interesting

textures. This adorable coat uses a mixture of rib and garter

stitch rows to create a stitch that looks almost as if it were

woven, not knitted. The resulting fabric is perfect for a spring or

fall coat. As the stitch is a combination of those you have already

used in this book, the project is much easier to knit than it might

look. Inspired by children's clothes from the forties and fifties,

this coat has a modern-classic design and shape.

gauge

20 sts and 28 rows to 4in. measured over woven-style pattern using Debbie Bliss Cashmerino Aran on size 8 needles, or the size required to give the correct gauge.

Always check gauge carefully and adjust needle size if necessary (see page 23).

measurements

TO FIT	6–12	12–18	18–24	24–36 months
CHEST	23	24½	26	28in.
LENGTH	12¾	13½	14	15in.
SLEEVE SEAM	6¼	7	8	8¾in.

back

Using size 8 needles, cast on 61(65:69:73) sts.

Work 8 rows in garter st.

CHANGE TO WOVEN-STYLE PATTERN

1st and 2nd rows: Sl 1, knit to end.

3rd row (RS): Sl 1, *k1, p1; rep from * to last 2 sts, k2.

4th row (WS): Sl 1, *p1, k1; rep from * to end.

These four rows form the woven-style pattern.

Continue in woven-style pattern until back measures 8(8¼:8¾:9)in., ending with a 4th row.

Next row (first decrease row) (RS): K2tog, k17(18:20:21), k3tog, k17(19:19:21), k3tog, k17(18:20:21), k2tog. *55(59:63:67) sts.*

Next row (second decrease row) (WS): K2tog, knit to last 2 sts, k2tog. *53(57:61:65) sts.*

Next row (RS): Sl 1, *k1, p1; rep from * to last 2 sts, k2.

Next row (WS): Sl 1, *p1, k1; rep from * to end.

SHAPE RAGLAN

Maintain continuity of woven-style pattern throughout.

Bind off 5(5:5:5) sts at beg of next 2 rows. *43(47:51:55) sts.*

Next row (RS): Sl 1, sl 1, k1, psso, rib patt to last 3 sts, k2tog, k1. *41(45:49:53) sts.*

Next row (WS): Sl 1, p1, rib patt to last 2 sts, p1, k1.

Next row: Sl 1, sl 1, k1, psso, knit to last 3 sts, k2tog, k1. *39(43:47:51) sts.*

Next row: Sl 1, p1, knit to last 2 sts, p1, k1.

Continue decreasing as established by the last four rows until 13(15:17:19) sts rem, ending with a WS row.

Bind off.

materials

4(5:6:6) 1¾oz (50g) balls of Debbie Bliss
   Cashmerino Aran in shade 205

Pair of size 8 knitting needles

Darning needle

4 large buttons

abbreviations

See page 39

left front

Using size 8 needles, cast on 42(45:48:52) sts. Work 8 rows in garter st.

CHANGE TO WOVEN-STYLE PATTERN

1st and 2nd rows: Sl 1, knit to end.

3rd row (RS): Sl 1, p1(0:1:1), *k1, p1; rep from * to last 2 sts, k2.

4th row (WS): Sl 1, k2, *p1, k1; rep from * to last 1(0:1:1) sts, p1(0:1:1).

These four rows form the woven-style pattern with 2 sts garter st front border. Continue in woven-style pattern until left front measures 8(8¼:8¾:9)in., ending with a 4th row.

Next row (first decrease row) (RS): K2tog, k21, k3tog, knit to end. *39(42:45:49) sts.*

Next row (second decrease row) (WS): Sl 1, knit to last 2 sts, k2tog. *38(41:44:48) sts.*

Next row (RS): Sl 1, p1(0:1:1), *k1, p1; rep from * to last 2 sts, k2.

Next row (WS): Sl 1, k2, *p1, k1; rep from * to last 1(0:1:1) sts, p1(0:1:1).

SHAPE RAGLAN

Maintain continuity of woven-style pattern with 2 sts garter st front border throughout.

Next row (RS): Bind off 5(5:5:5) sts, knit to end. *33(36:39:43) sts.*

Next row (WS): Sl 1, knit to end.

Next row: Sl 1, sl 1, k1, psso, rib patt to end. *32(35:38:42) sts.*

Next row: Sl 1, rib patt to last 2 sts, p1, k1.

Next row: Sl 1, sl 1, k1, psso, knit to end. *31(34:37:41) sts.*

Next row: Sl 1, knit to last 2 sts, p1, k1.

Continue decreasing as established by the last four rows until 22(24:26:30) sts rem, ending with a RS row.

SHAPE NECK

Maintain continuity of woven-style pattern with 2 sts garter st front border throughout.

Next row (WS): Bind off 13(15:17:19) sts, patt to last 2 sts, p1, k1. *9(9:9:11) sts.*

Next row: Sl 1, sl 1, k1, psso, patt to last 3 sts, k2tog, k1. *7(7:7:9) sts.*

Next row: Sl 1, k2, patt to last 2 sts, p1, k1.

Rep the last 2 rows until 3 sts rem, ending with a WS row.

Next row: Sl 1, sl 1, k1, psso.

Next row: k2tog.

Fasten off.

right front

Using size 8 needles, cast on 42(45:48:52) sts. Work 8 rows in garter st.

CHANGE TO WOVEN-STYLE PATTERN

1st and 2nd rows: Sl 1, knit to end.

3rd row (RS): Sl 1, k1, *p1, k1; rep from * to last 2(1:2:1) sts, p1, k1(0:1:1).

4th row (WS): Sl 1, k1(0:1:1), *p1, k1; rep from * to last 2 sts, k2.

These four rows form the woven-style pattern with 2 sts garter st front border. Continue in woven-style pattern until left front measures 8(8¼:8¾:9)in., ending with a 4th row.

Next row (first decrease row) (RS): K16(19:22:26), k3tog, k21, k2tog. *39(42:45:49) sts.*

Next row (second decrease row) (WS): K2tog, knit to end. *38(41:44:48) sts.*

Next row (RS): Sl 1, k1, *p1, k1; rep from * to last 2(1:2:1) sts, p1, k1(0:1:1).

Next row (WS): Sl 1, k1(0:1:1), *p1, k1; rep from * to last 2 sts, k2.

SHAPE RAGLAN

Maintain continuity of woven-style pattern with 2 sts garter st front border throughout.

Next row (RS): Sl 1, knit to end.

Next row (WS): Bind off 5(5:5:5) sts, knit to end. *33(36:39:43) sts.*

Next row: Sl 1, rib patt to last 3 sts, k2tog, k1. *32(35:38:42) sts.*

Next row: Sl 1, p1, rib patt to end.

Next row: Sl 1, k2, knit to last 3 sts, k2tog, k1. *31(34:37:41) sts.*

Next row: Sl 1, p1, knit to end.

Next row: Sl 1, rib patt to last 3 sts, k2tog, k1. *30(33:36:40) sts.*

Next row: Sl 1, p1, rib patt to end.

Next row (first buttonhole row) (RS): K3(3:4:4), bind off 4 sts, k2(3:4:5) [3(4:5:6) sts on right-hand needle after bind off], bind off 4 sts, knit to last 3 sts, k2tog, k1. *29(32:35:39) sts.*

Next row (second buttonhole row) (WS): Sl 1, p1, knit to buttonhole, cast on 4 sts, knit to next buttonhole, cast on 4 sts, knit to end. Maintaining continuity of woven-style pattern and raglan decreases, work 6(6:10:10) more rows in patt. *26(29:30:34) sts.*

Repeat the two buttonhole rows once more. *25(28:29:33) sts.*

Maintaining continuity of woven-style pattern with 2 sts garter st front border throughout, continue decreasing as established until 23(25:27:31) sts rem, ending with a WS row.

SHAPE NECK

Maintain continuity of woven-style pattern with 2 sts garter st front border throughout.

Next row (RS): Bind off 13(15:17:19) sts, patt to last 3 sts, k2tog, k1. *9(9:9:11) sts.*

Next row: Sl 1, p1, patt to end.

Next row: Sl 1, k2tog, patt to last 3 sts, k2tog, k1. *7(7:7:9) sts.*

Next row: Sl 1, p1, patt to end.

Rep the last 2 rows until 3 sts rem, ending with a WS row.

Next row: K2tog, k1.

Next row: K2tog.

Fasten off.

sleeves (both alike)

Using size 8 needles, cast on 23(25:27:31) sts. Work 6 rows in garter st.

CHANGE TO WOVEN-STYLE PATTERN

1st and 2nd rows: Sl 1, knit to end.

3rd row (RS): Sl 1, *k1, p1; rep from * to last 2 sts, k2.

4th row (WS): Sl 1, *p1, k1; rep from * to end.

These four rows form the woven-style patt.

Maintain continuity of woven-style pattern throughout.

Cont in patt, inc 1 st at each end of the next and every foll 4th(4th:6th:6th) row to 39(41:43:47) sts.

Cont in patt without shaping until sleeve measures 6¼(7:8:8¾)in., (or desired length to underarm) ending with a 4th row.

SHAPE RAGLAN

Maintain continuity of woven-style pattern throughout.

Bind off 5(5:5:5) sts at beg of next 2 rows. *29(31:33:37) sts.*

Next row (RS): Sl 1, sl 1, k1, psso, patt to last 3 sts, k2tog, k1. *27(29:31:35) sts.*

Next row (WS): Sl 1, p1, patt to last 2 sts, p1, k1.

Next row: Sl 1, knit to end.

Next row: Sl 1, p1, knit to last 2 sts, p1, k1.

Repeat these last 4 rows 2(2:2:1) times more. *23(25:27:33) sts.*

Next row (RS): Sl 1, sl 1, k1, psso, patt to last 3 sts, k2tog, k1. *21(23:25:31) sts.*

Next row (WS): Sl 1, p1, patt to last 2 sts, p1, k1.

Next row: Sl 1, sl 1, k1, psso, knit to last 3 sts, k2tog, k1.

Next row: Sl 1, p1, knit to last 2 sts, p1, k1.

Rep these four rows until 5 sts rem.

Bind off.

collar

Join raglan seams with mattress stitch, ensuring that the decreases can be seen to create a feature.

With RS facing and using size 8 needles, join yarn to neck edge and pick up and knit 6(6:6:8) sts up sloped right front neck, 4(4:4:4) sts from top of right sleeve, 15(17:19:21) sts across back neck, 4(4:4:4) sts from top of left sleeve and 6(6:6:8) sts down sloped left front neck. *35(37:39:45) sts.*

Work 16(16:18:20) rows in garter st.

Bind off (on WS).

Press collar lightly so that it folds back.

to finish

Sew side and sleeve seams. Weave in all ends. Attach buttons to left front to correspond with buttonholes. The fronts overlap across the bound off stitches at the front.

toys and accessories

patchwork blanket

A blanket can seem a daunting project to a beginner, with

seemingly acres of knitting to complete. However, this blanket is

very simple—just garter stitch—and is knitted in sections and

then sewn together. This means that you can knit a few squares

at a time between other projects or when traveling, without

having to carry around a mountain of yarn.

The final effect is of a beautiful, quaint patchwork blanket.

You can use as many or as few different colors as you wish,

depending on how you want your blanket to look.

materials

5 1¾oz (50g) balls of Debbie Bliss Cashmerino
    Chunky in shade 11 (yarn A)

2 1¾oz (50g) balls of Debbie Bliss Cashmerino
    Chunky in shade 02 (yarn B)

2 1¾oz (50g) balls of Debbie Bliss Cashmerino
    Chunky in shade 03 (yarn C)

2 1¾oz (50g) balls of Debbie Bliss Cashmerino
    Chunky in shade 10 (yarn D)

2 1¾oz (50g) balls of Debbie Bliss Cashmerino
    Chunky in shade 12 (yarn E)

Pair of size 10½ knitting needles

Darning needle

abbreviations

See page 39

This is a great project for practicing your finishing techniques, as there are many seams to sew up. If you find that your finishing is untidy to begin with, you may want to join the squares with blanket stitch, or another visible joining stitch, using a contrasting color yarn, in order to create a feature of the seams instead of trying to hide them.

gauge

14 sts and 25 rows to 4in. measured over garter stitch using Cashmerino Chunky on size 10½ needles, or the size required to give the correct gauge.

Always check gauge carefully and adjust needle size if necessary (see page 23).

measurements

Each square measures 4¾ x 4¾in.

Each edging strip measures 27½ x 4in.

Finished blanket measures 31½ x 31½in.

patchwork blanket

GARTER STITCH SQUARES

Make 5 squares in each of 5 colors, 25 squares in total.

Using size 10½ needles, cast on 17 sts.

Work 30 rows in garter st (every row knit).

Bind off.

GARTER STITCH EDGINGS

Make 4 strips in the color or colors of your choice.

Using size 10½ needles and yarn A, cast on 14 sts.

Work in garter st until strip measures 27½in.

Bind off.

to finish

Press all squares lightly to 4¾ x 4¾in.
Sew squares together, turning them
alternately so that each cast on or bound
off edge is attached to a row end edge.
This adds texture, with the garter ridges
alternating between horizontal and vertical,
and also helps ensure that all squares are
the same size, given that they can stretch
out of shape.
Sew the strips evenly around the edges of
the patchwork (see diagram on page 107).
Weave in all ends.

naming day blanket

This is a more delicate, pretty version of the Patchwork Blanket
and would make a gorgeous Naming Day shawl or gift for a new
baby. It's a slightly more advanced pattern, but as it's worked in
small squares, it's not difficult to handle. As you become more
skilled you can adapt this basic blanket pattern in several ways:
try working squares in different stitches or use different yarns.
If you do this, remember to knit gauge swatches so that you can
work out how big the individual squares will be.

This blanket is made in exactly the same way as the Patchwork Blanket, but uses different stitches for the squares and edging. If you like this version but don't want one color, then simply change colors for each square, as with the simpler pattern.

gauge

21 sts and 30 rows to 4in. measured over seed stitch using Cashmerino Aran on size 8 needles, or the size required to give the correct gauge.

14 sts and 27 rows to 4in. measured over lace pattern using Cashmerino Chunky on size 10½ needles, or the size required to give the correct gauge.

Always check gauge carefully and adjust needle size if necessary (see page 23).

measurements

Each square measures 4¾ x 4¾in.

Each edging strip measures 27½ x 4in.

Finished blanket measures 31½ x 31½in.

naming day blanket

SEED STITCH SQUARES

Make 13 squares.

Using size 8 needles and yarn A, cast on 25 sts.

1st row: K1, *p1, k1; rep from * to end of row.

This row forms the pattern.

Rep 1st row 34 more times. (35 rows in total.)

Bind off.

LACE SQUARES

Make 12 squares.

Using size 10½ needles and yarn B, cast on 17 sts.

1st to 4th rows: Knit.

5th row: K1, *yo, k2tog; rep from * to end of row.

6th to 8th rows: Knit.

9th row: K2, *yo, k2tog; rep from * to last st, k1.

materials

7 1¾oz (50g) balls of Debbie Bliss
   Cashmerino Aran in shade 001 (yarn A)
4 1¾oz (50g) balls of Debbie Bliss
   Cashmerino Chunky in shade 002 (yarn B)
Pair each of size 8 and size 10½
   knitting needles
Darning needle

abbreviations

See page 39

10th to 12th rows: Knit.

Rep 5th to 12th rows twice more.

29th row: As 5th row.

30th to 33rd rows: Knit.

Bind off.

SEED STITCH EDGINGS

Make 4 strips.

Using size 8 needles and yarn A, cast on 21 sts.

1st row: K1, *p1, k1; rep from * to end of row.

This row forms the pattern.

Rep 1st row until strip measures 27½in.

Bind off in seed stitch.

to finish

Press all squares lightly to 4¾ x 4¾in.

Sew squares together, alternating seed st and lace squares (see diagram, right).

Sew the strips evenly around the edges of the patchwork.

Weave in all ends.

building blocks

Knitting doesn't have to be used just for garments or

traditional baby items. Here is a fun pattern for blocks that can

be a great educational and enjoyable toy for a young baby.

The pattern is very easy and quick to knit, especially if you knit

only a few blocks, but you can make as many as you wish.

Just six balls of GGH Big Easy makes five multi-colored blocks,

but if you wish to make more blocks then buy an extra ball of

each color for every five extra blocks you wish to make.

The pattern calls upon the familiar format for making three-dimensional cubes out of six squares drawn on flat paper that many children learn at school. If you are unfamiliar with the technique, the diagram opposite will help.

gauge

17 sts and 22 rows to 4in. measured over stockinette stitch using GGH Big Easy on size 9 needles, or the size required to give the correct gauge.

Always check gauge carefully and adjust needle size if necessary (see page 23).

measurements

Each building block measures 4 x 4 x 4in.

a cube

For each cube use all the colors, one color for each of six 4 x 4-in. squares.

If making more than one block, change the color used for each square in the cube randomly.

When fastening off and joining in colors, leave a tail of yarn about 8in. long for sewing up.

MAIN PIECE (four joined squares)

Using size 9 needles and first color, cast on 17 sts.

Work 22 rows in st-st, starting with a knit row.

Fasten off first color.

Join in second color.

Work 22 rows in st-st, starting with a knit row.

Fasten off second color.

Join in third color.

Work 22 rows in st-st, starting with a knit row.

Fasten off third color.

Join in fourth color.

Work 22 rows in st-st, starting with a knit row.

Bind off.

SIDE SQUARES (make 2)

Using size 9 needles and fifth color, cast on 17 sts.

Work 22 rows in st-st, starting with a knit row.

Bind off.

Using size 9 needles and sixth color, cast on 17 sts.

Work 22 rows in st-st, starting with a knit row.

Bind off.

materials

1 1¾oz (50g) ball of GGH Big Easy in each of six
   colors: shade 13, shade 16, shade 19,
   shade 22, shade 24, and shade 25
Pair of size 9 knitting needles
Darning needle
Foam cubes each 4 x 4 x 4in.,
   or toy stuffing

abbreviations

See page 39

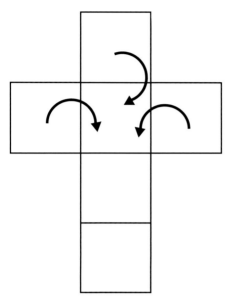

to finish

There are three pieces, a length with four
squares and two separate 4 x 4-in. squares.
All six shades of yarn should be used.
Press all sections lightly into shape.
Sew the two separate squares to either side
of the second square from the top of the
length (see diagram, above) using the tails
of yarn left to sew the seams.
Fold the squares along the lines where they
join another color. Pressing the folds will
help hold the cube's shape.
Fold in the top three squares first (see
diagram, above), and sew along all touching
edges with mattress st, with right side
facing outward.
Fold up the bottom two squares and sew
every seam except one with mattress stitch.
Push a foam cube (or enough stuffing to
make a firm cube without bulging) into the
center of the cube through the open seam.
Sew the last seam with mattress stitch.

bird mobile

A fantastic and fun way to use up scraps of yarn from other

projects and your stash. If you are a total beginner, use the yarns

recommended, but if you are growing in confidence, experiment

a little. The great thing about this project is that if the birds come

out in different shapes and sizes, it will add to their charm, so it

is not essential to get the gauge correct. Just follow the pattern

but remember to use the correct needle size for the yarn you

choose—check the ball band. And don't forget to use your artistic

license when sewing on the finishing touches!

materials

1 1¾oz (50g) ball of Debbie Bliss Cashmerino
   Aran in shade 602 (yarn A)

1 1¾oz (50g) ball of Debbie Bliss Cashmerino
   Chunky in shade 10 (yarn B)

1 1¾oz (50g) ball of Louisa Harding Kashmir DK
   in shade 02 (yarn C)

1 1¾oz (50g) ball of Louisa Harding Kashmir DK
   in shade 03 (yarn D)

1 1¾oz (50g) ball of Louisa Harding Kashmir DK
   in shade 05 (yarn E)

Pair each of sizes 6, 8, and 10½ knitting needles

Small size crochet hook

Stitch holder

Darning needle

2 x 12-in. long strips of plywood or other
   lightweight material. Do not worry about the
   thickness; anything you can find is fine, just
   make sure it is not too heavy.

Toy stuffing

Nail

abbreviations

See page 39

gauge

Not crucial for this project.

measurements

Each bird varies in size, but approx 6in.
from end of tail to tip of beak.

note

When making each section, use size of
needle relevant to yarn used.
Size 6 needles for Louisa Harding Kashmir DK.
Size 8 needles for Debbie Bliss Cashmerino Aran.
Size 10½ needles for Debbie Bliss
Cashmerino Chunky.

Make four birds for the mobile.
Mix the colors you use for each section
so that each bird is different.

body side 1

**Cast on 10 sts.
1st row (WS): Purl.
2nd row: Inc in first st, k7, inc in next st, k1.
12 sts.
Cont in st-st, casting on 2 sts at end of the
next row and 5 foll rows. *24 sts.*
Next row: Purl.
Next row: Inc in first st, knit to last 2 sts,
inc in next st, k1. *26 sts.*
Next row: Purl.
Rep last two rows twice more. *30 sts.*
Cont in st-st without shaping for 1½in.,
ending with a RS row.**

DIVIDE FOR HEAD AND TAIL
Next row (WS): P14 and leave these sts on
a stitch holder for head, bind off 6, p9.
10 sts on right-hand needle.
Work on these last 10 sts for tail.

Next row: K2tog, knit to last 2 sts, k2tog. *8 sts.*
Work 3 rows in st-st.
Next row: k2tog, knit to last 2 sts, k2tog. *6 sts.*
Work 3 rows in st-st.
Next row: K2tog, knit to last 2 sts, k2tog. *4 sts.*
Purl 1 row.
Next row: [K2tog] twice. *2 sts.*
Bind off.

HEAD
With RS facing, rejoin yarn to 14 sts left on
stitch holder.
Next row (RS): Knit.
Next row: Purl.
Next row: K2tog, knit to last 2 sts, k2tog.
12 sts.
Work 5 rows in st-st.
Next row: K2tog, knit to last 2 sts, k2tog.
10 sts.
Work 3 rows in st-st.
Next row: K2tog, knit to last 2 sts, k2tog.
8 sts.
Next row: Purl.
Next row: K2tog, knit to last 2 sts, k2tog. *6 sts.*
Bind off.

body side 2

Work as body side 1 from ** to **.

DIVIDE FOR HEAD AND TAIL
Next row: P10 and leave these sts on a
holder for tail, bind off 6, p13. *14 sts on
right-hand needle.*
Work on these last 14 sts for head.
Next row: Knit.
Next row: Purl.
Next row: K2tog, knit to last 2 sts, k2tog.
12 sts.
Work 5 rows in st-st.

Next row: K2tog, knit to last 2 sts, k2tog. *10 sts.*

Work 3 rows in st-st.

Next row: K2tog, knit to last 2 sts, k2tog. *8 sts.*

Next row: Purl.

Next row: K2tog, knit to last 2 sts, k2tog. *6 sts.*

Bind off.

TAIL

With RS facing, rejoin yarn to 10 sts left on stitch holder.

Next row: K2tog, knit to last 2 sts, k2tog. *8 sts.*

Work 3 rows in st-st.

Next row: k2tog, knit to last 2 sts, k2tog. *6 sts.*

Work 3 rows in st-st.

Next row: K2tog, knit to last 2 sts, k2tog. *4 sts.*

Purl 1 row.

Next row: [K2tog] twice. *2 sts.*

Bind off.

wings

Make two for each bird.

Cast on 4 sts.

1st row: Knit.

2nd row: Inc in first st, knit to last 2 sts, inc in next st, k1. *6 sts.*

Rep last 2 rows once more. *8 sts.*

Work 2 rows in garter st.

Next row: Inc in first st, knit to last 2 sts, inc in next st, k1. *10 sts.*

Rep last 3 rows twice more. *14 sts.*

Work 4 rows in garter st.

Next row: K2tog, knit to last 2 sts, k2tog. *12 sts.*

Knit 1 row.

Next row: K2tog, knit to last 2 sts, k2tog. *10 sts.*

Knit 1 row.

Bind off.

tummy

Make one for each bird.

Cast on 4 sts.

1st row: Knit.

2nd row: Inc in first st, knit to last 2 sts, inc in next st, k1. *6 sts.*

3rd row: Knit.

Rep last 2 rows once more. *8 sts.*

Next row: Knit.

Next row: Inc in first st, knit to last 2 sts, inc in next st, k1. *10 sts.*

Work 4 rows in garter st.

Next row: K2tog, knit to last 2 sts, k2tog. *8 sts.*

Work 2 rows in garter st.

Next row: K2tog, knit to last 2 sts, k2tog. *6 sts.*

Knit 1 row.

Rep last 2 rows once more. *4 sts.*

Bind off.

beak

Make one for each bird.

Cast on 8 sts.

1st row: Knit.

2nd row: K2tog, knit to last 2 sts, k2tog. *6 sts.*

Rep last 2 rows twice more. *2 sts.*

Bind off.

frame covers

Make 2.

Using size 10½ needles and chunky yarn, cast on 43 sts.

1st row: K1, *p1, k1; rep from * to end.

Repeating 1st row forms seed stitch.

Cont in seed st until fabric is long enough to go around the outside of the wooden lengths. Bind off.

Wrap covers around the wooden lengths and sew seams.

strings

Make 4 crochet chains with a small hook, or braid yarn to make strings. Do not use a single strand of yarn instead of crochet or braids, as this may not be strong enough to hold over time.

to finish

Press each piece lightly.

Weave in all ends.

Sew the two sides of body together with mattress stitch, starting at the bottom, sewing around, and leaving a hole in the bottom for stuffing. Stuff body with toy stuffing and sew up hole.

Sew on wings, beak, and tummy and embroider on eyes, tail feathers, and any other decoration you wish.

Attach the strings high on the back of each bird, so that the bird hangs straight and does not tip forward or backward.

Place one of the covered lengths of wood on the other at right angles to make a cross. Hammer a nail through the center to secure, then wrap lengths of yarn over and around the join to hold in place and ensure as little movement as possible.

Sew free ends of strings attached to birds to each free end of cross. You may wish to wrap the string around the wood as well, to take some strain off the fabric and prevent stretching the knitting when it is hanging. Finally, braid or crochet a chain about 8in. long to loop and attach to the top of the cross so that you can hang it from the ceiling. Of course, this hanging loop is optional and you may have alternative ideas of how and where to hang the mobile, depending on your own space.

special baby gift bib

A bib is not the first thing that comes to mind when thinking of a

project to knit for a baby, but it is a quick and easy one to make,

and a fun gift idea. The yarn used is machine-washable, durable

cotton, so it is practical and will deal with the dribbles and spills

of most weaning babies. It also looks incredibly stylish and is

much more comfy than the stiff plastic kind. However, do bear in

mind that, unlike the plastic kind, it does not wipe clean and so it

may be wise not to put it on junior when they are enjoying

cranberry juice or other highly staining foodstuffs!

materials

1 1¾oz (50g) ball of Debbie Bliss Cotton
    Cashmere in shade 26 (yarn A)
1 1¾oz (50g) ball of Debbie Bliss Cotton
    Cashmere in shade 32 (yarn B)
1 1¾oz (50g) ball of Debbie Bliss Cotton
    Cashmere in shade 07 (yarn C)
Pair of size 5 knitting needles
Darning needle
Approx 2-in. strip of hook and loop fastening

abbreviations

See page 39

gauge

22 sts and 30 rows to 4in. measured over stockinette stitch using Debbie Bliss Cotton Cashmere on size 5 needles or the size required to give the correct gauge. Always check gauge carefully and adjust needle size if necessary (see page 23).

measurements

LENGTH   12¾in.
WIDTH   8¾in.

bib

Using size 5 needles and yarn A, cast on 41 sts.

1st row (RS): K1, *p1, k1; rep from * to end.

2nd row: Inc in first st, p1, *k1, p1; rep from * to last 2 sts, inc in last st, k1. *43 sts.*

3rd row: P1, *k1, p1; rep from * to end.

4th row: Inc in first st, k1, *p1, k1; rep from * to last 2 sts, inc in next st, p1. *45 sts.*

Fasten off yarn A.

Join in yarn B.

5th row: K1, p1, k1, p1, knit to last 4 sts, p1, k1, p1, k1.

6th row: Inc in first st, p1, k1, purl to last 3 sts, k1, inc in next st, k1. *47 sts.*

7th row: P1, k1, p1, knit to last 3 sts, p1, k1, p1.

8th row: Inc in first st, k1, p1, k1, purl to last 4 sts, k1, p1, inc in next st, p1. *49 sts.*

Fasten off yarn B.

**Join in yarn C.

9th row: K1, p1, k1, p1, knit to last 4 sts, p1, k1, p1, k1.

10th row: K1, p1, k1, p1, purl to last 3 sts, k1, p1, k1.

Fasten off yarn C.

Join in yarn A.

11th and 12th rows: As 9th and 10th rows.

Fasten off yarn A.

Join in yarn B.

13th to 16th rows: Repeat 9th and 10th rows twice.

Fasten off yarn B.**

Rep stripe patt from ** to ** until bib measures approx 8in., ending with two rows yarn C.

SHAPE FRONT NECK

Maintain continuity of stripe pattern and seed st throughout.

1st row (RS): Seed st 4, k9, seed st 23, k9, seed st 4. *49 sts.*

2nd row: Seed st 4, p8, seed st 25, k8, seed st 4.

3rd row: Seed st 4, k7, seed st 27, k7, seed st 4.

4th row: Seed st 4, p7, seed st 4, leave these 15 sts on a holder, bind off 19 sts, seed st 3, p7, seed st 4. *15 sts on right-hand needle.*

Work on these 15 sts for left side of neck.

5th row (RS): Seed st 4, k7, seed st 4.

6th row (decrease row): Work 2 sts tog, seed st 3, p6, seed st 4. *14 sts.*

7th row: Seed st 4, k6, seed st 4.

Maintaining the continuity of stripe pattern with 4-st seed st borders, dec one st at neck edge on the next row and foll alt row. *12 sts.*

Work 3 more rows of patt without shaping, ending with a WS row.

SHAPE LEFT SIDE OF BACK NECK

Maintain continuity of stripe pattern and 4-st seed st borders throughout.

Next row (RS): Inc in first st, seed st 3, k4,

seed st 4. *13 sts.*

Next row: Seed st 4, p5, seed st 4.

Maintaining the continuity of stripe pattern with 4-st seed st borders, inc one st at neck edge on the next row and foll alt row. *15 sts.*

Next row: Seed st 4, p7, seed st 4.

Next row: Seed st 4, k7, seed st 4, cast on 22 sts. *37 sts.*

Next row: K1, *p1, k1; rep from * to last 11 sts, p7, seed st 4.

Next row: Seed st 4, k7, seed st to end.

Rep last two rows once more.

Next row: Seed st 4, purl to last 4 sts, seed st 4.

Next row: Seed st 4, knit to last 4 sts, seed st 4.

Maintaining the continuity of stripe pattern with 4-st seed st borders, rep last two rows until bib measures approx 12¼in., ending with 4 rows yarn B.

Fasten off yarn B.

Rejoin yarn A.

Next row: K1, *p1, k1; rep from * to end.

Rep last row 3 times.

Bind off in seed st.

SHAPE RIGHT SIDE OF NECK

Maintain continuity of stripe pattern and 4-st seed st borders throughout.

Rejoin yarn to right side of neck. Work as for left side of front neck and back neck, reversing all shapings.

to finish

Weave in all ends.

Press lightly.

Sew hook and loop fastening to back of neck to fasten bib.

rabbit soft toy

This delightful bunny is an easy toy to make and the yarn used

makes it safe to play with—no shedding of hairs, and it's

washable. Feel free to use the basic shape and play around with

the final look. The face can be stitched in different yarns or

colors, the ears can be made bigger or smaller, or a ribbon could

be tied around the neck. If you have older children, they may

wish to do some knitting and the scarf is a perfect way for them

to start. The project is not too big or daunting and doesn't need

a lot of time and concentration, so they won't get bored.

gauge

21 sts and 25 rows to 4in. measured over stockinette stitch using Debbie Bliss Cashmerino Aran on size 8 needles, or the size required to give the correct gauge.

Always check gauge carefully and adjust needle size if necessary (see page 23).

measurements

Height approx 10in.

body (makes 2)

Start at top of head.

Using size 8 needles and yarn A, cast on 6 sts

1st row (RS): Knit.

2nd row: Purl.

3rd row (increase row): *K1, inc in next st; rep from * to end. 9 sts.

4th row: Purl.

5th row (increase row): *K2, inc in next st; rep from * to end. 12 sts.

6th row: Purl.

7th row (increase row): *K3, inc in next st; rep from * to end. 15 sts.

Work 9 rows in st-st without shaping, ending with purl row.

17th row (decrease row): *K3, k2tog; rep from * to end. 12 sts.

SHAPE ARMS

Cast on 12 sts at beg of next 2 rows. 36 sts.

Cont in st-st without shaping for 1½in., ending with a purl row.

Next row: Bind off 9 sts, k17 (18 sts on right-hand needle), bind off next 9 sts and fasten off yarn. 18 sts.

With RS facing, rejoin yarn to body and work in st-st without shaping for 3in., ending with a purl row.

DIVIDE FOR LEGS

1st row (RS): K9, turn and leave rem 9 sts on holder.

Work on the first set of 9 sts.

Work 9 rows st-st, beg with a purl row.

Bind off.

Rejoin yarn to 9 sts left on a holder.

Work 9 rows st-st, beg with a purl row.

Bind off.

materials

1 1¾oz (50g) ball of Debbie Bliss Cashmerino Aran in shade 005 (yarn A)

1 1¾oz (50g) ball of Debbie Bliss Cashmerino Aran in shade 202 (yarn B)

1 1¾oz (50g) ball of Debbie Bliss Cashmerino Aran in shade 001 (yarn C)

Pair of size 8 knitting needles

Stitch holder

Darning needle

Toy stuffing

abbreviations

See page 39

OUTER EAR

Make 2.

Using size 8 needles and yarn B, cast on 8 sts.

Work 4 rows in st-st, beg with a knit row.

Next row (RS): Inc in first st, k5, inc in next st, k1. *10 sts.*

Work 3 rows in st-st without shaping.

Next row (RS): Inc in first st, k7, inc in next st, k1. *12 sts.*

Work 7 rows in st-st without shaping.

Next row (RS): Knit, dec 1 st at each end of row. *10 sts.*

Work 3 rows in st-st without shaping.

Next row (RS): Knit, dec 1 st at each end of row. *8 sts.*

Work 3 rows in st-st without shaping.

Next row (RS): Knit, dec 1 st at each end of row. *6 sts.*

Next row: Purl.

Next row (RS): Knit, dec 1 st at each end of row. *4 sts.*

Bind off.

INNER EAR

Make 2.

Using size 8 needles and yarn C, cast on 8 sts.

Work 4 rows in st-st, beg with a knit row.

Next row (RS): Inc in first st, k5, inc in next st, k1. *10 sts.*

Work 3 rows in st-st without shaping.

Next row (RS): Inc in first st, k7, inc in next st, k1. *12 sts.*

Work 3 rows in st-st without shaping.

Next row (RS): Knit, dec 1 st at each end of row. *10 sts.*

Work 3 rows in st-st without shaping.

Next row (RS): Knit, dec 1 st at each end

of row. *8 sts.*

Work 3 rows in st-st without shaping.

Next row (RS): Knit, dec 1 st at each end of row. *6 sts.*

Next row: Purl.

Next row (RS): Knit, dec 1 st at each end of row. *4 sts.*

Bind off.

TUMMY PANEL

Using size 8 needles and yarn C, cast on 4 sts.

1st row: Knit.

2nd row: Inc in first st, k1, inc in next st, k1. *6 sts.*

3rd row: Knit.

4th row: Inc in first st, k3, inc in next st, k1. *8 sts.*

5th and 6th rows: Knit.

7th row: Inc in first st, k5, inc in next st, k1. *10 sts.*

Work 8 rows in garter stitch without shaping.

15th row: Knit, dec 1 st at each end of row. *8 sts.*

Work 2 rows in garter stitch without shaping.

18th row: Knit, dec 1 st at each end of row. *6 sts.*

19th row: Knit.

20th row: Knit, dec 1 st at each end of row. *4 sts.*

Bind off.

SCARF

Using size 8 needles and yarn B, cast on 4 sts.

1st and 2nd rows: Knit.

Drop yarn B.

Join in yarn C.

3rd and 4th rows: Knit.

*Drop yarn C.

Pick up yarn B.

5th and 6th rows: Knit.

Drop yarn B.

Pick up yarn C.

7th and 8th rows: Knit.

Repeat from * until scarf measures approx 10in., or length required, ending with 2 rows of yarn B.

Bind off using yarn B.

to finish

Weave in all ends that will be visible.

Sew together both sides of body all around the edges, leaving a gap in the top of head for stuffing.

Stuff, then thread a length of matching yarn through the edge all around gap left in top of head and pull up tight to draw in. Secure and fasten off.

Thread matching yarn in and out of sts all around neck and pull tight to draw in the neck further.

With WS facing, sew inner ears to outer ears then attach ears to top of head.

Attach tummy panel.

Using yarn C, make a small (about 1½in. diameter) pompom and attach this to rabbit's behind.

Embroider a smiley face and claws with leftover yarn or with scraps of other color yarns you may have in your stash.

Tie scarf around neck.

caring for garments

Handmade items need special care and knitted ones are no different, even if the yarns used in this book are machine-washable. The fact that the yarns are a special blend of natural and synthetic means that you don't have to treat them as delicately as pure wools, as they are unlikely to felt and shrink to nothing, and will hold their shape better, but they are still prone to stretching and pulling, like any other knitted garment. With more delicate items that are for "Sunday best," like the Naming Day Blanket, you may wish to hand wash, regardless of the washing instructions on the ball label. However, all items should where possible be washed on a delicate or cool wash and avoid the final spin in the machine, as they are prone to becoming misshapen, especially when wet.

Instead of a spin, when the garment is removed from the machine it should not be wrung, but placed on a dry towel. Roll up the towel with the garment inside as pictured and apply pressure to squeeze out excess water without pulling it out of shape. You may feel that you need to do this a few times, but when the garment is less sodden, you can then lay it out flat to dry on a dry towel. Knitted garments do not like to be hung; gravity does its worst and the article of clothing can stretch out of shape. This is why you should not clothes pin it to a clothes line, especially as pins will also leave stretch marks in knitting. When dry, you can use a cool steam iron to smooth the item out, but do not apply pressure, as this will flatten the yarn and stitches. Finally, fold and place the garment in a drawer or cupboard, away from the moths!

suppliers

Contact the distributors listed
for your local yarn stockist.

UNITED STATES

DEBBIE BLISS YARNS
Knitting Fever Inc
315 Bayview Avenue
Amityville
New York 11701
Tel: 516 546 3600
Fax: 516 546 6871
Web: www.knittingfever.com

GGH YARNS
My Muench Yarns
1323 Scott Street
Petaluma
California 94954-1135
Tel: 707 763 9377
Fax: 707 763 9477
Web: www.muenchyarns.com

LOUISA HARDING YARNS
Knitting Fever Inc
315 Bayview Avenue
Amityville
New York 11701
Tel: 516 546 3600
Fax: 516 546 6871
Web: www.knittingfever.com

ROWAN YARNS
Westminster Fibers
4 Townsend Avenue
Unit 8
Nashua
New Hampshire 03063
Tel: 1-800-445-9276
Web: www.westminsterfibers.com

CANADA

DEBBIE BLISS YARNS
Diamond Yarns Ltd
155 Martin Ross Avenue
Unit 3, Toronto
Ontario M3J 2L9
Tel: 416 736 6111
Fax: 416 736 6112
Web: www.diamondyarn.com

GGH YARNS
Muhlenstrasse 74
D-24521 Pinneberg
Germany
Europe
Tel: 04101 208484
Fax: 04101 208551
Web: www.ggh-garn.de

LOUISA HARDING YARNS
Diamond Yarns Ltd
155 Martin Ross Avenue
Unit 3, Toronto
Ontario M3J 2L9
Tel: 416 736 6111
Fax: 416 736 6112
Web: www.diamondyarn.com

ROWAN YARNS
Diamond Yarns Ltd
155 Martin Ross Avenue
Unit 3, Toronto
Ontario M3J 2L9
Tel: 416 736 6111
Fax: 416 736 6112
Web: www.diamondyarn.com

conversions

MEASUREMENTS

If you are converting from one
system of measurement to
another, convert every instance
of it in the pattern. Do not work
partly in metric and partly in
imperial or discrepancies
between the measurement
systems may occur.

INCHES TO CENTIMETERS
Multiply the figure in inches by
2.45 to obtain the
measurement in centimeters.

YARDS TO METERS
Multiply the figure in yards by
0.9144 to obtain the
measurement in meters.

OUNCES TO GRAMS
Multiply the figure in ounces
by 28.57 to obtain the weight
in grams.

KNITTING NEEDLE SIZES

US	METRIC	OLD UK
0	2mm	14
1	2.25mm	13
	2.5mm	
2	2.75mm	12
	3mm	11
3	3.25mm	10
4	3.5mm	
5	3.75mm	9
6	4mm	8
7	4.5mm	7
8	5mm	6
9	5.5mm	5
10	6mm	4
10½	6.5mm	3
	7mm	2
	7.5mm	1
11	8mm	0
13	9mm	00
15	10mm	000

index

acknowledgments

I must extend my warm thanks and appreciation to everybody who
contributed to creating the beautiful *Easy Baby Knits*, my first book.
Firstly to the dedicated team, especially Alison, Pamela, and Rachel,
who have created a wonderfully clear and handsome book.
Claire Richardson's gorgeous photography has captured exactly the spirit in which the knits
were designed and, along with Pamela, her styling of the wonderfully sweet models brings
the garments to life. Which brings me to the children—many thanks to Skye, Noah, Yana,
Charlotte, Maya, Zhene, Adam, Oliver, and Kai, and special love to Gemma and Finley.
Deepest thanks go to Pauline Hornsby, my wonderful pattern checker, and Kate Haxell,
my knitting editor, who have both worked meticulously to iron out the creases.
A heartfelt thank you goes to Cheryl, Annie, my family, and the companies who supplied
yarn and accessories: Susan at loop, Sue at Get Knitted and Jane at Designer Yarns.
Finally, all my love and thanks to Sean, who encouraged me to stick with knitting!